Registration Methods for the Small Museum

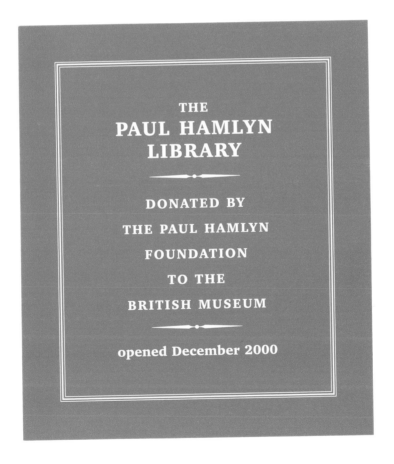

ABOUT THE SERIES
The American Association for State and Local History Book Series publishes technical and professional information for those who practice and support history, and addresses issues critical to the field of state and local history. To submit a proposal or manuscript to the series, please request proposal guidelines from AASLH headquarters: AASLH Book Series, 1717 Church St., Nashville, TN 37203. Telephone: (615) 320-3203. Fax: (615) 327-9013. Web site: www.aaslh.org.

ABOUT THE ORGANIZATION
The American Association for State and Local History (AASLH) is a non-profit educational organization dedicated to advancing knowledge, understanding, and appreciation of local history in the United States and Canada. In addition to sponsorship of this book series, the Association publishes the periodical *History News*, a newsletter, technical leaflets and reports, and other materials; confers prizes and awards in recognition of outstanding achievement in the field; and supports a broad education program and other activities designed to help members work more effectively. To join the organization, contact: Membership Director, AASLH, 1717 Church St., Nashville, TN 37203.

Registration Methods for the Small Museum

Fourth Edition

Daniel B Reibel

ALTAMIRA
PRESS

A DIVISION OF
ROWMAN & LITTLEFIELD PUBLISHERS, INC.
Lanham • New York • Toronto • Plymouth, UK

ALTAMIRA PRESS
A division of Rowman & Littlefield Publishers, Inc.
A wholly owned subsidary of The Rowman & Littlefield Publishing Group, Inc.
4501 Forbes Boulevard, Suite 200, Lanham, MD 20706
www.altamirapress.com

Estover Road, Plymouth PL6 7PY, United Kingdom

British Library Cataloguing in Publication Information Available

Library of Congress Cataloging-in-Publication Data

Reibel, Daniel B
  Registration methods for the small museum / Daniel B Reibel. — 4th ed.
      p. cm. — (American Association For State And Local History Book series)
  Includes bibliographical references and index.
  ISBN-13: 978-0-7591-1130-1 (cloth : alk. paper)
  ISBN-10: 0-7591-1130-8 (cloth : alk. paper)
  ISBN-13: 978-0-7591-1131-8 (pbk. : alk. paper)
  ISBN-10: 0-7591-1131-6 (pbk. : alk. paper)
   1. Museum registration methods. I. American Association for State and Local
History. II. Title.
  AM139.R44 2008
  069'.52—dc22

069. 52   REI

                                                                  2007046825

Printed in the United States of America

∞™ The paper used in this publication meets the minimum requirements of
American National Standard for Information Sciences—Permanence of Paper
for Printed Library Materials, ANSI/NISO Z39.48-1992.

Contents

~

Introduction to the Fourth Edition

There has been a revolution since I wrote the first edition of this book in 1977. Then there was a better than even chance that the museum would not have a paid staff, and if it did the people were untrained. It is quite likely that the museum would not even have a good typewriter. Computers were around, but only a few museums had access to them. There was some technical literature but the whole published knowledge of the museum field could be grasped in one hand. There were lots of paper and lots of forms. Museum accreditation had started in 1970, but there were few universal standards.

Now many museums will have a professional staff and the staff is not only well trained but well read as well. I have about four feet of bookshelf space in museum-related books, and I do not buy everything that comes out. One would have to do some searching to find a typewriter to buy, and the computer reigns supreme. Paper has not been eliminated, but what paper there is, is ancillary to the function of the electronic system. Forms have gone the way of the typewriter to be replaced by screens in a computer program. The accreditation program has created a national standard for museum practice. The AAM has a department that does nothing but try to oversee and improve standards and the profession is living up to them. This book has to reflect these changes.

Readers may wonder, in the computer age, why there is so much on paper records in this book. There is a good chance that any museum with collection records dating back more than ten years may have extensive paper records in their files. Museums need to print paper records from time to time. Also, the old paper files need to be archived in case there is a question.

Why a Registration System?

The operative words in the title of this book are "Registration Methods" and "Small Museum." Taking them in order I will try to explain why I wrote this book.

Your collection is not a museum until it has an adequate registration system. The intention of this book is to give you the tools necessary to have as good a registration system as the largest museum in the country. Indeed, a small museum may have a better registration system than the largest museum because the size of the collection is comprehensible.

I hope that this book helps define a registration system, what it ought to do, and how to achieve a real registration system, one that will withstand the scrutiny of the most meticulous accreditation team.

Small Museum

No one has ever successfully defined a small museum. The Small Museums Committee of the Mid-Atlantic Association of Museums once defined a small museum as one with a lone professional, but I have been in many museums with several professionals who thought of themselves as small.

Even the smallest museum now has access to a computer that gives them potential to do things of extraordinary sophistication, particularly when compared with museum registration systems of even ten years ago. I thought that if I could help the small museum use the potential of modern practices it would further the goal of every museum having a well-registered collection.

Small need not mean poorly run. Small may mean that the size and complexity of the collection can be grasped very easily, and of a dimension where even a small staff can handle it. From my experience with accreditation visits and MAP surveys I can assure you that some large museums cannot always say the same. I thought that a book that would give the small museum a reachable goal was what was required.

The author's experience is all in history museums and this will give the book a slant, but I think this book will be useful to any professional. There are differences between types of museums. History collections are large, like some science collections, but history museums need to store lots of data, like art museums. Science museums have a better taxonomy than history museums, and art museums hardly need a classification system at all. Other than that, the need to be able to preserve information, track the collection, and account for one's actions is the same for any type of museum.

Sometime in 1975, at a meeting at Colonial Williamsburg, Paula Degan asked me the difference between the registration systems of an art, science, and history museum? I did not know, but went home and thought about it and eventually wrote her describing the differences between several types of museums that I use in chapter 1. The outgrowth of this question was the first edition of this book.

When I discussed the differences between registration methods for different types of museums, I realized that almost all the literature on museum registration was written for art museums. Not only that, but there was very little other material on "professional" subjects in print. I thought my book would correct that condition. When I was writing the first edition of this book, I had a chance to read Robert Chenhall's book while it was in page proofs. I thought that this book would give museums another tool to raise standards. Whether Chenhall or I contributed anything to it, standards are certainly higher today than they were in 1977.

All of the examples used in this book exist and are from my own observation. For example, when I use the illustration of a schoolhouse at one end of the county and a mansion at the other, they exist, and I have visited them and looked at their collections.

The forms that are not printed in the text are in appendix A. The forms are referred to by their number, i.e., A-6 for the sixth form in appendix A.

I would like to thank the late Bill Alderson for encouraging me to publish the first edition, and, of course, my wife, Patricia, who kept me at it.

Daniel B Reibel

CHAPTER ONE

~

Why Have a Museum Registration System?

Most institutions do not have a corporate history that goes back beyond the memory of their most long-term employee. Tax records may have to go back as far as seven years, budgets may track three years, but most records seldom last much longer than a year. This is in marked contrast to museum collection records that theoretically last forever. The history of the object in the collection is an important component of it and sometimes more important than the object itself.

The museum registration system is the museum's memory. Long after curators and registrars have come and gone, the records of the museum will speak. In keeping the historical story straight they are as important as the object itself. A museum that fails to keep good records fails in its primary function; some would say its only function. With good records, more than the object is preserved. With poor records, something more valuable than the object itself may be lost.

The person, or persons, in charge of a museum have been given a trust. They have been placed in charge of a collection for a short period of time. It is their obligation and duty to see that the collection is well cared for and that it is passed on to the next caretakers in as good a condition as when they received it. Good care includes good records. Good record keeping does not have to be difficult, time consuming, or costly.

There are collections of furniture, beer-bottle caps, art, matchbook covers, glass, ceramics, insulators stolen from telephone poles, seashells, animals, pornography, and so on. A museum may collect one or several of these things and more, but not all collections are museums. A museum has several characteristics that separate it from a mere collection. The American Association of Museums once had these criteria for a museum that wishes to be accredited:

- Has a collection that is educational or aesthetic in nature
- Has a full-time professional staff person who has experience and knowledge of the current standards and practices
- Presents regularly scheduled programs and exhibits that use and interpret objects
- Has a formal and appropriate collection documentation and follows standards in the care and use of the collections
- Has a formal and appropriate program of maintenance and presentation of exhibits

Volunteer-run museums may not have a professional staff member but can meet the other criteria.[1]

Private collections lack some or all of these characteristics. The American Association of Museums once defined a museum for accreditation purposes as ". . . an organized and permanent nonprofit institution, essentially educational or aesthetic in purpose, with a professional staff, which owns and utilizes tangible objects, cares for them, and exhibits them to the public on some regular schedule."[2]

Notice the statement that the museum owns and cares for its collections. For accreditation purposes, care has been defined as protecting the essential integrity of the object and being able to account for it. The caring for collections is the essence of the difference between being a museum and not being a museum. The records are considered an important part of the object. Most museums that fail to be accredited fail accreditation because of the kind of care given their collections. Many of such failures come about because of inadequate or incomplete records. A museum will be considered a good museum if the staff maintains good records, but it may not be considered a museum at all if that is not done.

Over the years the museum field has developed a record-keeping system that is now pretty standard and consistent enough to be applied to widely different circumstances of each museum collection. The system is actually quite simple. There is not much mystery to it, nor is there a need to invent your own record-keeping system.

How a History Museum May Differ from Other Kinds of Museums

There are differences between types of museums, and these are often reflected in their record-keeping procedures.

I must define the term "specimen" to make the rest of this discussion clearer. This term helps explain the difference among museums better than any other. It comes from a Latin root meaning "a distinguishing mark," with the idea that the object stands out. Technically speaking, any object in a museum collection is a specimen. However, in the narrower use of the term, as often used in the museum field today, a specimen is an object that represents any other object in its class or type. It may be the best example, but it is still just representative. To some museums any specimen can easily be replaced by another, and better, one. Some museums separate their specimens from their collection, and even give the specimens a lower standard of care. This concept of the object as a specimen is not universal in the museum field, nor even popular, but it is something to keep in mind.

The major difference between a history museum and other museums is that we collect objects that have some historical association attached to them. This historical association makes the object valuable all out of proportion to its value as a specimen or its monetary value. *It cannot be replaced by a better specimen.* Other characteristics of history museums are that the collection is of man-made objects, tends to be large, and is monetarily valuable. History museums share many of these characteristics with art and anthropology collections, but normally a history museum is the only type of museum where the major collecting effort is of objects with historical associations.

Registration systems in museums have to be flexible enough to account for these conditions and be able to record a lot of data on many objects.

Definitions
It is important to understand the terms used in this book, so I am listing some of them. My definitions are not exactly those of a dictionary, but they show the way these terms are commonly understood in the museum field today:

Accession: An accession is an object or a group of objects in the museum collection obtained at one time from a single source. The act of accessioning is taking possession and title to the object, placing it in the museum collection, and making a record of it.

Catalogue: A catalogue is a reference tool created by arranging some of the collection records in categories.

Collection: A museum collection is a group of objects kept together for some reason. Usually the relationship is due to similarities in the nature of the objects, their being collected by an individual or group, or their association with a person, place, or event. A collection may have only a few pieces in it, or it may have thousands. A museum may contain one collection or several collections.

Collection Manager: See Registrar.

Curator: The definition of this term has been narrowed in the last few years, but for the purposes of this book the word means the professional person in charge of a collection. The collection may be the whole museum or only part of it. In some museums today the curator may be responsible for research and someone else, such as the registrar or collection manager, is responsible for the collection.

Director: The person in charge of the museum. This term recognizes that the museum is not only its collections but also its program. The director is not only in charge of administration but the museum's professional program as well.

Documentation: This is the factual information gleaned about each object in the collection. Some of this information is developed by examination of the object and some is acquired by research. In some applications the term "documentation" applies to all the records in the registration system.

Museum: This is an institutionalized collection, the records of that collection, the physical plant where this collection is housed, and one that is potentially accreditable as a museum by the American Association of Museums.

Register: For our purposes, the register is a list of the accessions, loans, etc., of the museum in some logical order.

Registrar: This is the person in charge of the museum's registration system. In the past few years the responsibilities of the registrar have been broadened to include extended responsibilities over the whole area of collection policy and management. In fact, the term "collection manager" is beginning to replace registrar in some museums as the preferred term. In museums without a registrar, the curator(s) or the professional staff is responsible for the records.[3]

Registration: This is the whole process of creating, acquiring, and keeping the records on a museum collection and is the subject of this book.

The person who is actually doing the registration should start with the attitude that registration is just one of the tasks to be performed so that some of the other tasks, such as acquiring more objects, preserving existing objects, and interpreting the collection, can be accomplished.

Boundaries

Policies have a way of affecting practices and it is a good idea to make sure your policies are in order before developing practices. The first thing needed for a good registration system is a firm set of boundaries for the museum. This is found in the museum's statement of purpose and mission statement. These two are commonly combined into what is often called the mission statement. The mission statement should discuss what the museum is and what it is going to do.

Hero County Historical Society

(*purpose*)

What Is the Museum?

The Hero County Historical Society is a nonprofit educational association

And Its Purpose Is?

that collects, preserves, and interprets the history of Hero County, Franklin,

For What Time Period?

for the period of the arrival of the first Native Americans in this region until the present day, with special emphasis on the period since the founding of the County (1785) until the end of the 19th century (1900),

(*mission*)

By What Means?

by the collection of books, documents, artifacts, and other cultural objects, preserving them, and interpreting them to the public by means of a museum, educational programs, lectures, public events, and publications

Any Other Qualifications?

and to encourage others to collect, preserve, and interpret the history of Hero County and do everything worthwhile to carry out our purpose.

Written as a paragraph, the statement would look like this:

MISSION STATEMENT
   Hero County Historical Society
   The Hero County Historical Society is a nonprofit educational association that collects, preserves, and interprets the history of Hero County, Franklin, for the period of the arrival of the first Native Americans in this region until the present day, with special emphasis on the period since the founding of the County (1785) until the end of the 19th century (1900), by the collection of books, documents, artifacts, and other cultural objects, preserving them, and interpreting them to the public by means of a museum, educational programs, lectures, public events, and publications, and to encourage others to collect, preserve, and interpret the history of Hero County and do everything worthwhile to carry out our purpose.

This is a good mission statement since it confines the museum to the collection of only those objects related to the history of the county. Within that limit it is very broad, as it allows the museum to collect almost everything.

As the museum's operation grows and changes over the years, the purpose will probably not change much, but the mission will become more and more complex. Large museums will have mission statements that cover several pages. It is not unknown for a museum to rewrite their mission statement every time they develop a new long-term plan, say every five years. For the small museum, a simple mission statement, like the one above, will be perfectly adequate.

Before developing a collection policy, the museum should carefully examine its statement of purpose to see if it defines the kind of collection the museum wants. In the case of the Hero County Historical Society it would not limit the museum enough. This museum would want to develop a collections management policy statement that further defines the museum's mission:

COLLECTIONS MANAGEMENT POLICY

HERO COUNTY HISTORICAL SOCIETY

What Type of Objects Will the Museum Collect?

It is the policy of the Hero County Historical Society to collect only those objects made and/or used in Hero County, or are associated with a person, place, or event in the County, or, to a limited extent, are typical or representative of objects made or used in the County;

What Is the Scope of the Collection?

and that are historical, cultural, or aesthetic in nature;

Is There a Limit on the Period of the Collection?

that cover the period from 1785 to 1900;

Are There Any Other Limits?

and for which the museum has an ultimate use and for which the museum can care under standards acceptable to the museum field at large.

Written out as a paragraph, this statement would look like this:

COLLECTIONS MANAGEMENT POLICY

HERO COUNTY HISTORICAL SOCIETY

It is the policy of the Hero County Historical Society to collect only those objects made and/or used in Hero County, or are associated with a person, place, or event in the County, or, to a limited extent, are typical or representative of objects made or used in the County; and that are historical, cultural, or aesthetic in nature; that cover the period from 1785 to 1900; and for which the museum has an ultimate use and for which the museum can care under standards acceptable to the museum field at large.

This statement defines the collection a little more narrowly than the statement of purpose. The object should have a direct association with some person, place, or event in the county, but there is a clause allowing the museum to collect "representative" objects. The museum cannot collect seashells since they were not made or used in the county and are not historical, cultural, or aesthetic in nature. The museum cannot collect a locomotive, unless it will have some use for it and can take care of it. These conditions may not be too confining and they will keep the museum's collection activities concentrated on what it really needs and can care for.[4] The enforcement of such a policy will help prevent problems with deaccessions later.

These collection management policies keep the museum focused on what it is really trying to do. Before you develop any collection manual you should make sure that your policies define a method of reaching your goals and that everyone understands them.

Collection Management Policy Manual

All the policies and procedures that affect the collection should be brought together in a collection management policy manual. The reason for having a manual is that there will be a consistent set of practices through several curatorial administrations. It is important that the manual reflect actual operating practices, be usable by anyone, and be short and easy to read. Collection management polices are not stagnant documents. They need to be reviewed annually and updated when needed.

Even the smallest museum needs legal advice on exactly how the whole collection policy should be handled. It is a good idea to have the museum's whole collection policy looked over by a good lawyer.

The procedures carry out the policy, and may require certain practices that affect policy. The manual should include both policies and procedures. The board should be involved in developing the manual and in carrying out its provisions. There are two sample collection management policies in the appendix.

What Does a Registration System Do?

After coming this far in the chapter I should at least explain what a museum registration system does. The registration system is a system of policies, procedures, practices, and documents that provides a link between the objects and their history and insures that

- The museum's right of ownership of the object is established.
- Associations with a person, place, or event are preserved.
- Interpretation of the object is enhanced.
- Preservation of the object is aided.
- The museum can identify and account for every object in the collection.

In order to do all these things the museum must have a well-developed collection policy and a set of procedures to carry it out.

The Rule and Its Test

There is a Rule that should apply to any museum registration system. That Rule is:

Any registration system used by a museum should be readily understandable to any intelligent but uninformed layman using the registration system itself, without any human assistance.

The museum does not need a high priest or priestess to interpret a divinely inspired registration system to the benighted masses below. What is needed is a system that anyone can understand in the event that the curator is not there to explain it.

The Test of any system is:

- The museum should be able to produce any object from its collection from any document picked at random from its registration system.
- The museum should be able to produce all the documentation for any object picked at random from its collection.

If your museum cannot pass The Test, keep working on the problem until you can. I have seen large museums with large professional staffs that cannot pass The Test and small volunteer-run museums that can.

Who Bells the Cat?

There is almost always a board or governing body responsible for the museum. That group has the ultimate responsibility for the collection. The board decides who is actually going to do the work.

In a museum with a professional staff, the decision is much easier: the professional staff does the work. The board has delegated its responsibility for the area of the museum to the professional staff and those persons, among other things, are responsible for the records. It does not matter how large the staff is, if the curator or director is the only paid professional, that person is responsible. In situations where there is more than one professional, the director may delegate responsibility. If the museum is fortunate enough to afford it, there will be a registrar, but do not get the chain of responsibility confused. The governing body is responsible and delegates its authority to the professional, who may further delegate it. If something goes wrong, it is the professional's responsibility. If the governing body allows the error to continue, it is its responsibility. With apologies to Lewis Carroll, what I have told you three times is true.

In the case of the volunteer-run museum, the governing board not only has the responsibility, but also has to do the work. In that event, there is usually a person or group of persons willing to undertake the care of the collections. This person or group assumes the functions of curator and registrar. This office may be incorporated into a collections or museum committee. The committee takes charge of the registration system and reports to the governing body on its activities from time to time. These volunteer-run museums can have very effective records. Whether run by volunteers or professionals, a museum can have the kinds of records it wants. If the people involved in the museum have a commitment to a good registration system they will have it, whether or not there is a professional on the staff. Unfortunately, the opposite corollary is also true.

The collections committee of the governing body offers an extra bit of continuity and responsibility to the collection, and can make the transition from one curator to another or from one administration to another, more easily than it would otherwise be. For these reasons, I feel that museums should have some committee to oversee its collections whether or not the museum has a professional staff.[5]

Where to Start

The ideal situation is not to have a previously registered collection at all so you can start from scratch. New organizations are actually very fortunate in this respect. A new organization can develop a registrar's manual before it ever acquires a single object and can have an accurate and complete registration system from the beginning.

Museums that already have collections may not be so lucky. If your collection has been well cared for and you have good records, you are probably reading this book for the fun of it. If your collection has not been taken care of, and the records are a mess, you have a problem to solve before you do anything else. (See figure 1.)

What to Do about Bad Documentation

I would suggest that any museum starting with disorganized collection records should start with a computer. After the initial start-up, it is easier, quicker, and a lot cheaper to use than any manual system, but it also takes a lot of planning and a large commitment on the part of the museum to carry out the job. See chapter 8 on computers.[6]

If your museum has a poorly catalogued collection, your first task is to get it into shape. It is difficult to tell someone how to do this without actually seeing the collection, but there are some things that can be done with any collection.

Assemble All the Records

The first task is to assemble all the records you have and try to sort them out. Think of yourself as an auditor with a terrible bookkeeping system that has to be straightened out, particularly as the IRS is on its way. If you only sort the records you have by year, you will have a good start. Try to match correspondence related to your collection with objects listed in your files. If anyone was around when the mess was created, try to get them to advise you. Ask anyone who is familiar with the museum what they know about the col-

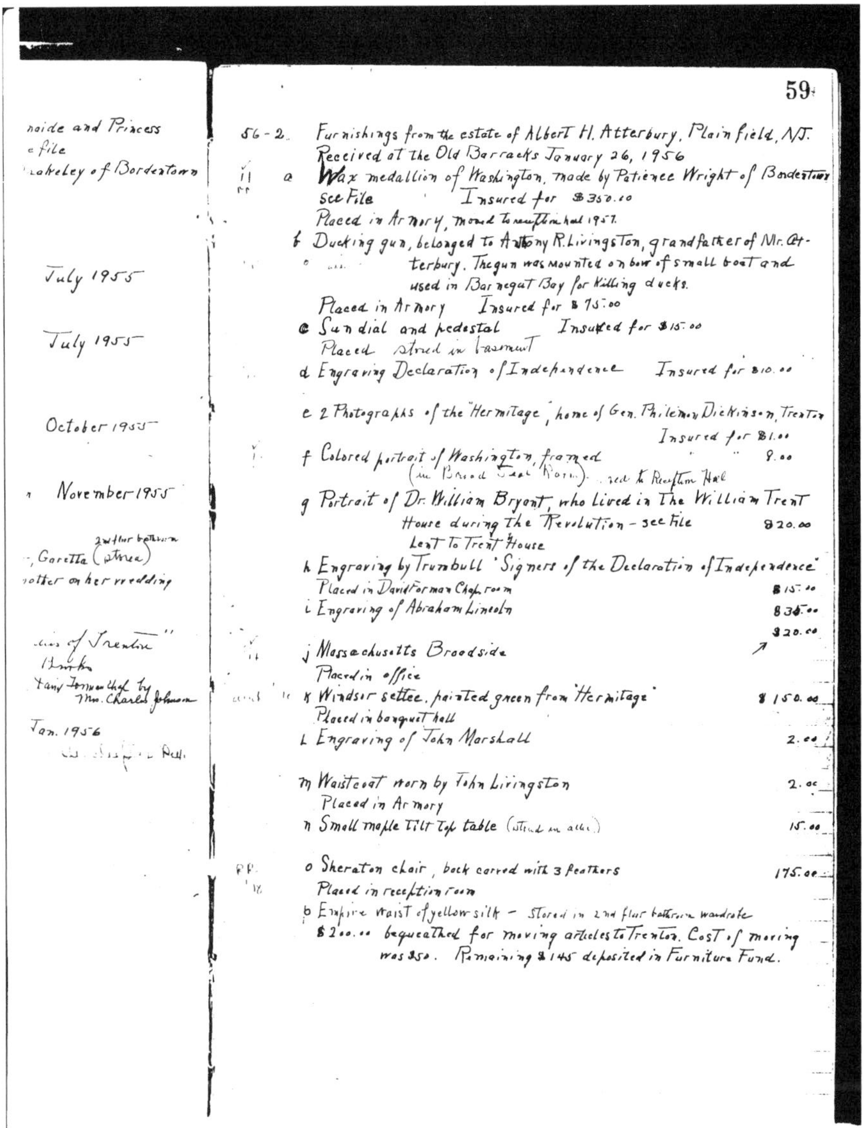

59

...noide and Princess
...e file
...Lakeley of Bordentown

56-2. Furnishings from the estate of Albert H. Atterbury, Plainfield, N.J.
Received at the Old Barracks January 26, 1956

a Wax medallion of Washington, made by Patience Wright of Bordentown
see File Insured for $350.00
Placed in Armory, moved to reception hall 1957.

b Ducking gun, belonged to Anthony R. Livingston, grandfather of Mr. Atterbury. The gun was mounted on bow of small boat and used in Barnegat Bay for killing ducks.
Placed in Armory Insured for $75.00

July 1955

c Sundial and pedestal Insured for $15.00
Placed stored in basement

July 1955

d Engraving Declaration of Independence Insured for $10.00

e 2 Photographs of the "Hermitage", home of Gen. Philemon Dickinson, Trenton Insured for $1.00

October 1955

f Colored portrait of Washington, framed " " 8.00
(in Board [illegible] Room) ... to Reception Hall

November 1955

g Portrait of Dr. William Bryant, who lived in the William Trent House during the Revolution - see File $20.00
Lent to Trent House

...Goretta (stored) 2nd floor bathroom
...mother on her wedding

h Engraving by Trumbull "Signers of the Declaration of Independence"
Placed in David Forman Chap. room $15.00

i Engraving of Abraham Lincoln $30.00
$20.00

...of Trenton"
[illegible]

j Massachusetts Broadside
Placed in office

[illegible] by Mrs. Charles Johnson

k Windsor settee, painted green from "Hermitage" $150.00
Placed in banquet hall

Jan. 1956

l Engraving of John Marshall 2.00

m Waistcoat worn by John Livingston 2.00
Placed in Armory

n Small maple tilt top table (stored in attic) 15.00

o Sheraton chair, back carved with 3 feathers 175.00
Placed in reception room

p Empire waist of yellow silk - Stored in 2nd floor bathroom wardrobe
$200.00 bequeathed for moving articles to Trenton. Cost of moving was $50. Remaining $145 deposited in Furniture Fund.

Figure 1: Page from Bound Ledger Kept until 1991. Most museums kept similar ledgers until after the Second World War. Whatever weaknesses this format has, it kept data in order, usually in the order received. Courtesy of the Old Barracks Museum.

lection. Look at old board minutes. Write letters to people who have moved. Just remember the old system made sense to someone at some time; try to figure out their reasoning, no matter how disorganized that may be, and you have won half the battle.

Make a Register
The written information must be in some usable form. I suggest making a register of the old records by accession number. (See figure 2.) When you find an accession number this will quickly lead you to the right data. If there are catalogue cards you can arrange them by the title of the object. That will give you two ways to find something, either by number or title. Computer records can be indexed into some useful form.

Don't Move Anything
Do not move any objects until you have their present locations firmly fixed in the records and your mind. Objects are often left in one location in the museum for long periods of time, even decades. The relationship of the object to its location may be preserved in the records or the memory of someone associated with the museum.

Make an Inventory
It is a good idea to make an inventory of the museum before you move anything. Do one room at a time, making a short description of *everything* in the room. All objects found in the museum when the new registration system is set up should be noted. If the objects have numbers, make a register of them. A video camera is one way to record the locations of objects before inventory.

In many respects a computer file is a lot easier to use than a card file. For instance, you can search for all the tables 43 to 46 inches long and have a chance of finding the 45-inch table you are looking at. On the other hand you will have to be inventive as the computer in a simple search may not be able to find a library table mislabeled as a dining table, and measurements can be inaccurate. The computer can generate a catalogue by number, title, and location if the information exists. These are very useful in inventories.

After you have fixed the location of each object try to put the records for all of one type of object together. If you have all the tables together, a description such as "one old table" may suddenly have meaning.

If the Collection Is Numbered
If the collection is numbered try to reconcile that with the records. The logic of the system will become clearer when you do this. I have found in these sit-

OLD BARRACKS MUSEUM
Collections Register

Year: 1956

Number	Object	Source	Comment	L	C	I	Loc
56.1A	RUG	MRS ELIZABETH B. CASE	ORIENTAL, SMALL			✓	COL STOR
56.1B	"	"	"			✓	COL STOR
56.1C	"	"	"			✓	COL STOR
56.1D	"	"	"			✓	COL STOR
56.1E	"	"	"			✓	
56.1F	"	"	"			✓	COL STOR
56.1G	"	"	"			✓	COL STOR
56.1H	"	"	"			✓	COL STOR
56.1I	"	"	"			✓	
56.1J	"	"	"			✓	
56.2A	MEDALLION WAX, GW	EST. ALBERT ATTERBURY				✓	BOX 93
56.2B	GUN MARKET	"				✓	COL STOR
56.2C	SWADDLE + PEDESTAL	"				✓	
56.2D	ENGRAVING PRE	"				✓	
56.2E	PHOTOGRAPHS "HERMITAGE"	"				✓	
56.2F	PORTRAT GW	"				✓	
56.2G	DR. JOHN BRYANT	"				✓	
56.2H	ENGRAVING, SIEWERS DOT	"	BY TURNBULL			✓	
56.2I	A LINCOLN	"				✓	
56.2J	BROADSIDE, MASS.	"				✓	
56.2K	SETTEE	"	WINDSOR			✓	
56.2L	ENGRAVING, JOHN MARSHALL	"				✓	BOX 105 COL STOR
56.2M	WAISTCOAT	"				✓	
56.2N	TABLE, TILT TOP	"	MAPLE			✓	BOX 32
56.2O	CHAIR, FEATHERED SPLAT	"	SHERATON			✓	
56.2P	WAIST (DRESS?)	"	EMPIRE			✓	
56.3A	LEDGER	GERALD PIDCOCK	STACY POTTS 1766			✓	BOX 192
56.3B	"	"	POTTS + NANCY 1872			✓	BOX 167
56.4	CHAIR, LADDERBACK	J.D. OLIPHANT	CONVENT L39.19 TO GIFT			✓	COL STOR
56.5	SECRETARY	PURCHASE	CHIPPENDALE, MAHOGANY			✓	OF ACC.
56.6	SLEEVE LOOSE	OBA	WORN BY MARIA EVERNMAN			✓	BOX 16
56.7	DRESS FRAGMENT		WEDDING			✓	BOX 24
56.20	SIDE CHAIR	EST. ALBERT H. ATTERBURY	SHERATON				

uations, the numbers on the objects usually bear a reasonable relationship to the numbers in the records. I have found it easiest to make a register of the numbers from the records and check these off as I find the objects. That way I avoid duplications. You will also find numbered objects that bear no apparent relationship to the records.

If the numbering system is completely disorganized, you may have to use a combination of techniques dealing with both numbered and unnumbered collections.

Do not assume that just because the object is marked with an accession number that it has been accessioned. Conversely, if the object is not numbered, it may yet have been accessioned.

If the Collection Is Not Numbered

If the collection is not numbered you should assign numbers during the inventory. It is difficult to advise anyone on how this is to be done without seeing the collection records, but these rules apply to almost all situations. You should take steps to see that

1. The fact the objects are not numbered should be preserved in the numbering system.
   a. If the objects have a known status (i.e., a known provenance or source) you would assign numbers to objects in the same fashion you would for any other accession.
   b. If the objects are of unknown provenance then you accession them as one big group.
      (1). You can assign an artificial year of accession. If you are working in 1996 all the items of unknown provenance are accessioned as if in the year 1995. That is, any object numbered 94.XX.XX is of unknown provenance. If the previous year has been used in your registration system, use system (2).

or

      (2). You can assign an artificial donor or source number, perhaps the number 1 (one). With this system, if you are working in 1996, all the accession numbers 96.1.XX are of unknown provenance. This is the method I prefer to use instead of an artificial year.

2. You must keep a very accurate register of what you have done.
3. You must place the accession number on each object as it is accessioned.

How to Reconcile the Completed Catalogue
You will end up with three classes of objects:

a. Objects that can be related to the records.
b. Objects that cannot be identified from the records.
c. Records that are not related to any object.

The tendency is to assume that unidentified objects do not have records and that the loose records refer to missing or stolen objects. Before these assumptions are made, carefully try to match the records with the objects. My experience has been that many of the objects thought to be "missing" actually exist in the collection, but that the records are too disorganized to identify them. Some pretty strange descriptions creep into the files. I have seen measurements off by as much as a foot, beds described as stands, cider presses described as lard presses, and so on. After you have carefully compared the records with the objects, you will have to admit that some discrepancies have crept into your records. These discrepancies can be "resolved" by reaccessioning the objects.

Never Throw Out Old Records
Never throw out old records, no matter how confused they are. Even if the records are completely disorganized, someone in the future may want some information from them. Never discard the old numbering system. Even if you renumber everything you should carefully note the old numbers in the new records. The old numbers may be referred to in your registration documents.

If There Are No Records
If there are no records you must treat the collection as a single accession. You can use the same techniques as you would in an unnumbered collection.

Be Complete and Consistent
The reason the old registration methods may be a mess is often that whoever was keeping them was not consistent and did not complete what they set out to do. If you do not want someone to curse the day you were born, you must complete what you start, and you must be consistent. That means you must account for every object and reconcile all problems in the records. It is better to do one section of the old collection at a time, and do it well, than to try to do it all and be unable to complete what you start. Even if you are not using the most efficient procedures your consistency and completeness will make the system useful.

Be Cautious about Reaccessioning
And finally, if you have a problem, reaccessioning is not always the way to solve it. You can end up with several registration systems. It is better to salvage the old system in order to preserve much of the original character of your records. A good way to salvage the old system is to catalogue it. See chapter 6.

Make a Record of What You Have Done
Write down an exact description of what you have done and make sure this gets preserved in your records. I would recommend binding it in the front of the accession ledger for the years you updated the records, or place it in your procedural manual.

What you are trying to do is make sure that those who come after you understand what you did and why. It is too much to expect someone to understand the basic logic of your actions without some explanation. I have seen dozens of collections where someone "renumbered" or "recatalogued" it in some illogical and incomplete fashion, leaving no record of what they did or why, and creating a tremendous mess that causes problems for interminable periods of time afterwards. If they had left a short explanation, it would have made things easier on the rest of us.

Volunteers and Registration
Museum professionals differ about using volunteers in general, and using them in registration in particular. There is some negative feeling, and volunteers tend to be used mainly in the areas of interpretation and program. Volunteers can be very useful in the area of registration if the professional staff give some training and set realistic, specific goals and work with them.

Collectors and knowledgeable people might be willing to catalogue your collection in their area of interest. Bottle collectors might work with your bottle collection, stamp collectors with your stamps, gun collectors with your weapons, and so on. If you can tap that source of expertise, you can tap a whole community of interest that can help the museum with exhibits, publications, and collections, and who can also steer valuable information into your collection. The computer is ubiquitous in our society and many people have sophisticated backgrounds in computers and can give you real assistance.

I, personally, find volunteers very useful, their knowledge helpful, and their enthusiasm rewarding. I would not run a museum of any size without them.

Ethics
Morals are private but ethics are public.

A legal friend once advised me never to do anything, no matter how innocent, that I would not mind discussing in open court. For ethics, that is a good rule to follow. Ethics codes usually urge people to avoid even the appearance of impropriety, and the museum collection is one area where that is a sound practice. The Accreditation Commission insists that all museums being accredited adopt an institutional code of ethics. Whether you intend to be accredited or not, it is a good idea to have one.

The museum field has evolved a consensus on ethics and has developed a number of ethics codes. The board ought to formulate such a code considering several factors discussed here.[7] A statement about ethics appears in the sample collection policies in the appendix.

It is not a good idea for the board member or the staff to be in the actual business of privately collecting, buying, and selling in the same area in which the museum's collection falls. These people in posts of trust or honor should avoid going into competition with the museum. People interested in the museum, and curators trained in its field of interest, will, as a matter of course, be knowledgeable about areas similar to that of the museum's collection and may privately own objects which could be in that collection. They may buy and sell from their own collection from time to time. They should inform the board if they have substantial holdings. If an object that should be in the museum's collection is offered to one of these persons, the person should offer the museum first refusal. If one of these privileged persons sells some of their own collection, they should offer it to the museum first. As a practical matter, the small museum will seldom be in a position to buy one of these objects, but knowledge of the transaction keeps everything visible so the board can be informed and make judgments wisely.

A knowledge of the marketplace is desirable in a curator. Many great collections have been built by a collaboration between a curator and dealers. On the other hand, it is undesirable for the curator or board member to operate an antiques shop or to be a partner, silent or otherwise, in one or to have a similar conflict of interests. I personally do not collect in the same area as the museum at which I work, but it is pertinent to remember that for other curators and board members to do so may be desirable. If there is a potential conflict, the board should set up a mechanism where everything is out in the open, so neither party is injured, but under which both can operate.

A colleague of mine once had to discuss the price she expected to pay for an object to be auctioned at a board meeting in front of a board member who was going to bid against the museum! You do not want to be in that situation.

Conclusion

The first steps, then, are important. The museum should decide that it is going to have a good registration system and set out to do what is necessary to achieve it.

- It is as important to know why you are doing something as it is to know how to do it.
- It is important to stay within definite boundaries.
- It is even more important to be consistent and to complete each process before going on to the next step.
- It is important to get all the information you can on each object and file it where it can be found.

That sounds like a lot to do, but the consequences of not doing it will take more time than doing everything on this list well.

Notes

1. These criteria are a paraphrase of the AAM's definition of a museum from about 1970. Another criterion was that the museum had to be open on a regular and predictable basis.

2. *Museum Accreditation: A Handbook for the Institution* (Washington, DC: American Association of Museums, 1990), 26. An official of AAM pointed out to me that this definition is for accreditation purposes only.

3. Mary Case, ed., et al, *Registrars on Record: Essays on Museum Collections Management*, Registrars Committee (Washington, DC: American Association of Museums, 1988). Rebecca A. Buck and Jean Gilmore, "Collection Terminology," *New Museum Registration Methods* (Washington, DC: American Association of Museums), xiv–xv, 13–23, 98, has an outline of a job description for a registrar. The word "curator" or "collections manager" do not appear in the index, or, so far as I can discover, in the text.

4. There are numerous discussions of collection policies. See John E. Simmons, *Things Great and Small: Collection Management Policies* (Washington, DC: American Association of Museums, 2006); Marie C. Malaro, *A Legal Primer on Managing Museum Collections*, 2nd ed. (Washington, DC: Smithsonian Institution, 1998), 43–51; a useful outline of Ms. Malaro's ideas appears in "Collections Management Policies," in Anne Fahy ed., *Collections Management*, Leicester Readers in Museum Studies

(New York: Routledge, 1995), 11–28, with a sample collection policy; less useful is Marilyn Phelan, *Museums and the Law*, Volume 1 (Nashville, TN: AASLH, 1982), 94ff ; More theoretical is James B. Gardner and Elizabeth E. Merritt, *The AAM Guide to Collection Planning* (Washington, DC: American Association of Museums, 2004).

5. The use of a collection committee is not a standard practice in the history museum field, but, in my opinion, it should be. See especially Malaro, *Primer*, loc. cit.

6. This section was delivered as an address by the author before a session of MAAM meeting in Washington, DC, 1994; Rebecca A. Buck and Jean Allman Gilmore, *Collection Conundrums* (Washington, DC: American Association of Museums, 2007), 24–31.

7. Weisz, Jackie, compiler, Roxana Adams, series editor, *Codes of Ethics and Practice of Interest to Museums* (Washington, DC: American Association of Museums, 2000); Karol Schmiegel, "Professional Ethics," in Buck and Gilmore, *New Museum Registration Methods*, 277–280. The quote about ethics being public was once a common saying in the museum field. I have not heard it lately but it is true more often than not.

CHAPTER TWO

~

Acquisition

The first stage of the registration process is the acquisition of the object. This process starts with the first contact with the owner of the object. Someone may approach the museum with an item they wish to donate or sell, or the museum may approach them. Museums acquire objects mainly by two methods, as gifts and as purchases, but other methods include exchange, bequests, transfer from one museum collection to another, and collection in the field. Any documents created by this contact, particularly letters, bills of sale, and notes, become the first items in your accession file.[1]

Acquiring Title

The most important thing about these first steps in the registration process is that the museum gets actual title and possession of the object and a document proving that the museum owns it. You would be amazed at the number of museums that cannot prove they own their collections. Title passes to you when you acquire all the rights of ownership, that is the right to do anything that the museum wants to do to the object.

In order to pass good title to you the person transferring the object must have good title themselves. They must have an unrestricted right to the object and be free to give or sell it to the museum. The museum should question the owner on that right. There is a considerable difference between acquiring an object that has been in a family for generations, and buying it from some unknown dealer off the back of a truck. In the case of gifts, the museums should make sure that there is not some other person in the family with an interest in the object. You cannot acquire an object from a juvenile without parental permission, and even this may come into question when the juvenile reaches majority.

In gifts the first steps that the museum takes should insure that it acquires these rights:

- The right to display or not display the object as the museum pleases. If the museum is bound to display something permanently, that would bind them to one kind of exhibit forever.
- The right to break up collections. If the museum is given a collection of household objects, it might be expedient to store the glassware in one place and the ceramics in another, rather than keeping it all together. The museum may wish to keep the collection in the general ledger. The museum may wish to keep only part of the collection and dispose of the rest.
- The right to dispose of the object as the museum sees fit. Although the museum does not intend to dispose of any of its collection, there are times when it has too many of one thing and can trade or sell them and should not be restricted from doing so.

It is better to acquire all these rights at the beginning and not have to worry about them later.

These rights of property may sound harsh to a prospective donor, but the donors themselves would not want to own property with any restrictions on it, and neither does the museum. Contrary to what these rights imply, the museum is under a heavy responsibility to keep everything it acquires. Museums that "churn" their collections inevitably get into trouble.[2]

Copyright
Keep in mind that certain rights may not belong to the owner. The most ordinary ones would be copyright or trademark. You can pretty much assume that if the copyright is not specifically transferred to you in writing you do not own it. The law on copyrights is very complex. Copyright notices do not have to be placed on objects after January 1, 1978. Trademarks expire periodically but some are kept alive long after the original company that owned them has gone out of business.[3]

NAGPRA and the Nazis
The Native American Graves Protection and Repatriation Act (NAGPRA, 1990) affirms the right of Native Americans and Native Hawaiians to cus-

tody of their human remains, funerary and sacred objects, and objects of cultural patrimony *that are in the control of federal agencies and museums*. If you have such objects in your collection you may be under an obligation to return them. If the object was collected on federal land or was from a protected grave site NAGPRA may apply. NAGPRA has become a sort of ethical code for anthropology museums. You should be aware that any Native American artifact should have provenance that does not put it under NAGPRA.[4] You never can acquire good title for stolen goods so examine provenance carefully.

From just before and during World War II (1938–1945) The Nazis stole huge amounts of artwork and cultural items from individuals, museums, and governments. Very little of that has been returned, but that does not mean the original owners lost all their rights. Any work of art with a shaky provenance during the war years is suspect.

Before you even borrow, let alone buy, an object with a questionable provenance you should check with police. The FBI has a large division that does nothing but tract stolen art.

As an example, it is one thing to establish a good provenance for an item that has been in a family for generations and which may not have a single piece of paper as evidence. It is another question where a similar piece may have a very vague provenance.

Purchases

It is simpler to acquire the necessary rights with things you buy but not so simple with gifts. When a museum purchases something, it gets a bill of sale. If there is a willing seller who has unobstructed title to the object, a willing buyer, an exchange of equal value, and all the other processes of the marketplace, then you almost always have a clear title to the object. The bill of sale and all other documents of the transaction should be marked with the accession number of the object and placed in the accession file.[5]

Even the smallest museum needs legal advice on exactly how such purchases should be handled. It is a good idea to have the museum's whole collection policy looked over by a good lawyer.

Gifts

Most museums of any size depend on gifts of objects to make up their collections. When someone gives an object to the museum and the transaction is without value received, but only for goodwill, the museum's title to the object is not as clear as it is for a purchase. A gift normally passes absolute ownership from the givers to the recipients only when there is the intention to make the gift and free will on the part of the givers, something they, or their heirs, can deny later.

To help establish their title to gifts, museums should have donors sign a "transfer-of-title form" or "gift agreement form." The gift agreement is pretty clear evidence of free will and the intention to make a gift.[6] The actual donor will seldom, if ever, claim his or her property back. I have never had it done to me in fifty years in the museum business, although I know of cases where it has happened at other museums. In these cases, incidentally, the museums refused to return the objects and were upheld. Never, ever, accept a gift without a properly executed gift agreement form. In the absence of any preliminary documents, that will be the first document in the museum's accession file on that particular accession. Such a form should clearly state that the donor is giving up all rights and title to the object. A statement on such a document might be

I/We _____ hereby give to the trustees of the XYZ Museum absolute and unconditional ownership of the following , together with all copyright (in all media by any means now known or hereafter invented) and any associated rights which I/we have.[7]

The transfer of title should clearly state what is being given, show the date of the transaction, and provide a place for the signatures of the donor and a representative of the museum. In some states you may need a witness to the signature. With this statement, the description of the property, and all the signatures, you have a good claim to the object, but the title may not be absolute, and the watchful museum professional keeps that in mind.

A gift of an object to a history museum collection places an obligation on the museum. This obligation is to preserve the object and to keep all historic associations. Although these obligations are seldom mentioned, or placed in writing, they are usually assumed by the donor: "You're a museum, after all." Donors and communities become very upset when the museum does not live up to these expectations. There are several court cases where museums have been held remiss for failing to perform these unwritten obligations. That places a heavier load on gifts than on purchases, though this rule applies to the whole collection.

If the donor gives you money to buy something, the object purchased is a gift. You still have to get a bill of sale or a receipt for the purchase, but the accession is actually a gift. Because the donor gave you money, the object is much more clearly the property of the museum than the gift of the object it-self might be, but objects purchased in this way should be treated as any other gift. Since you already have a document transferring the object, you may not need a gift agreement form in these cases, but should have some document from the donor indicating the gift.

With bequests to the museum, the executor or the lawyer handling the estate, will usually supply some document, such as a copy of a portion of the will, or something similar. In many cases he will only produce a letter stating that he is executing the will and has the power to transfer the property to the museum. These documents are usually sufficient to establish title to the object and you will not need a gift agreement signed, but every time this comes up check with your lawyers.

Occasionally you will be bequeathed items with restrictions on them. These restrictions might include the way the bequest is to be acknowledged ("In Memory of B. Knott Forgotten"), but also might include the donation of objects you do not want or restrictions on the bequest, such as requiring that it be kept together in a collection or permanently exhibited. Each instance must be handled individually, but the institution must be careful not to place itself in the position of not being able to break up collections or of always having to exhibit some particular object. You are not in a position to negotiate with the donor. If you accept the object from a bequest, you may have to keep it permanently, unlike other portions of your collections. In these cases, your lawyer can advise you.

Sometimes heirs to an estate will give items in memory of the deceased. These are not bequests from the estate, but are gifts from the heirs, and have to be treated like any other gift.

Museums also acquire objects by law. Objects are turned over to the museum in the normal legislative process. One is surplus goods from a government unit. Another example would be the Hero County Civil War battle flags being turned over to the Hero County Historical Society by action of the county commissioners. Some objects, such as archives, are sometimes turned over automatically by law. It would be a good idea, mandatory, as a matter of fact, to get a signed letter of transmittal for such a gift. A receipt may be good enough here, but you can never get enough legal advice, so ask your lawyer.

There are "collections in the field." This term usually applies to archaeological and scientific collections, but history museums also acquire objects in this fashion. Salvaging something from a junk pile might be the closest analogy to scientific field collection. If you get to salvage machinery from a factory that is to be torn down, that too is collection in the field. You should have some document showing you had the right to do this, and that the items collected are yours. Collections in the field are handled as any other accession.

Museums exchange objects with other museums and institutions, or give and receive transfers of objects. These deals are usually done on a friendly basis, but, again, you should have a document showing you have title. In the absence of any other document, the transfer-of-title form should be sufficient documentation. Usually each museum will send copies of its accession file with the exchange. Transfers and exchanges are handled as any other accession or deaccession.

It is not a good idea to accept an object on loan pending its donation as a gift. Some flexibility may have to be exercised here, as the museum may wish to examine it before accepting it, or the authorizing person may not be available. There is a method of doing this which is often called by the clumsy title "deposit loan." A deposit loan is a short-term loan (usually less than thirty days) that the museum takes in under much lower standards of care than other loans. The museum usually does not agree to any responsibility, other than to guard against gross negligence, and places all the responsibility for the delivery and pickup on the lender. These loans have to be tracked very carefully, and cleared as early as possible. Deposit loans are discussed further in chapter 7.

Possession of the Object

Warning flags should go up whenever the owner does not want to give possession. Title to the object, and possession of it, are two different things at law, but for practical purposes, you may assume that you do not have title unless you also have possession. In the case of gifts, title passes only with possession, particularly when there is a tax consideration. It would be difficult to imagine a valid purchase without the museum acquiring possession. There are, however, situations occasionally where possession of an object does not immediately pass to the museum. These deals should not be consummated without the advice of a lawyer and a discussion with the board.

There are "partial" gifts where the museum shares ownership with another museum or person. In these cases the museum owns only a certain percentage of the object, and has possession only a portion of the time. Partial gifts are very difficult to handle. The number of potential problems is infinite. To have a partial gift in storage is ridiculous and I would recommend not accepting partial gifts unless it is an object you just have to have, and which will add significantly to your exhibits.

There are gifts where the owner may retain certain rights. An example would be a famous person retaining the right of publication of his or her papers. This is something to approach carefully, but if you must accept something with this kind of restriction, put a time limit on it. Ten to twenty-five years is reasonable, or perhaps terminating on the donor's death.

A museum has to be careful about giving "life tenure" or long-term possession to the donor on objects in the collection. This is particularly true when a tax deduction is involved. The donor usually cannot claim tax deductions unless the title to the property has been transferred and the object itself is in the possession of the museum. You may have trouble getting such property away from the heirs. Museums are usually not in a position to engage in long and expensive lawsuits. The original owner seems to live forever.

At this point, whether it was a purchase or a gift, the object is now in the possession of the museum, and you have title to it. If you do not, go back to Go and start again.

Acknowledgment of Gifts

It is an excellent idea to acknowledge all gifts, both privately and publicly. There are several ways to do this. Many organizations have a printed form which they send to the donor to acknowledge a gift. That is adequate, but I prefer a personal letter. A gift is a declaration of faith in the museum and deserves more than a form letter. It takes very little effort to make each one personal. (See figure 3.)

The person who receives this letter will know you really appreciated the gift. Notice the accession number on the lower left. A copy of this letter and of Mrs. Donor's letter of inquiry asking the museum if it wants the collection are placed in the accession file. All of these documents, along with the public display of the objects as gifts, may prove the museum's claim to title in the future if the heirs should claim that auntie didn't know what she was doing when she gave away the spoons.

A good place to acknowledge a gift publicly is in your newsletter. It will give good publicity among people most interested in the museum and will encourage them, too, to give. Another place is a new-accessions exhibit in some good corner of the museum. This will be seen by the casual visitor.(See figure 4.)

If the item is exhibited, the label should acknowledge it as "Gift of Mrs. Deductible Item," or, in the case of a fund, "Purchased by the Faith, Hope and Charity Fund." This is important, and the donors, their family, and their friends, will receive a great deal of satisfaction from seeing the name on the label. If the name is left off, the donor and potential donors may

```
┌─────────────────────────────────────────────────────────────┐
│            THE HERO COUNTY HISTORICAL SOCIETY                 │
│               The John A. Hero Mansion                        │
│               804 East Lincoln Avenue                         │
│                 Hero, Franklin 20123                          │
│                                              July 6, 2008     │
│  Mr. B. Generous Donor                                        │
│  26339 York Road                                              │
│  Hero, Franklin 21123                                         │
│                                                               │
│  Dear Mr. Donor:                                              │
│                                                               │
│      I wish to thank you for the gift of the one-wheeled      │
│  automobile. The museum de-pends on the generosity of         │
│  donors to develop our collection and we appreciate the       │
│  trust you have placed in the museum in making this           │
│  donation. It is an important ad-dition to the collection     │
│  and will be enjoyed by our visitors for years to come. You   │
│  can see it on display in the Carriage House.                 │
│                                                               │
│      Would you be good enough to sign the enclosed gift       │
│  agreement form and return it to us in the enclosed envelope. │
│                                                               │
│      I wish to thank you for the gift on behalf of the Board  │
│  of Trustees of the Hero County Historical Museum.            │
│                                                               │
│                                      Sincerely,               │
│                                                               │
│                                      P. Bismarck Adams,       │
│                                      Director                 │
│                                                               │
│  008.21                                                       │
└─────────────────────────────────────────────────────────────┘
```

Figure 3:   A Typical Thank-You Letter. Notice the accession number on the bottom of the letter. This ties the object to the documents.

quite rightly think that you do not care. That is public evidence that the object was a gift. Publication of gifts in your newsletter is also a public announcement of the gift. All this publicity of the object as a gift helps document the museum's claim to it. Courts have ruled that the public display of an object with the unchallenged statement that it is a gift is evidence of the donation.

Some donors don't want their name used publicly. The reasons for this are various, but usually involve the donors not wanting the public to know they owned such an object. They fear becoming targets for thieves or ungrateful relatives. You should honor this request when asked. Privacy laws limit the

Accessioned Donations

George Akel: lifeboat oar from the Liberty ship
  Ambrose E. Burnside, 1945.
Margaret M. Baham: hats & clothing worn by her aunt,
  Ethel Bernard, 1920s-40s.
Brenda Bailey: stereo console & 45 RPM records, 1970.
H.P. Bell: scuppernong wine made & bottled in
  Pender Co., 1993.
BMS Architects: 6 bottles unearthed on site of former
  Chamber of Commerce building, early 1900s.
Bladen Lake State Park: 4 turpentine pans used to
  collect rosin, 1940s.
Charles H. Boney, Jr.: ferry station blueprint, 1920s-30s.
Leslie N. Boney, Jr.: Azalea Festival poster (Bellamy
  Mansion), 1991.
Sylvia Bowles: sign, doctor's bag & medications from
  Dr. Daniel C. Roane, 1940s.
Helen K. Chandler: 2 lamp post lamps from garage at
  711 Market St., c. 1900-10.
City of Wilmington: newspaper supplement on
  downtown Wilmington revitalization, 6/16/65.
Nancy Faye Craig: prom dress, crinoline, gloves, shawl,
  sash, apron & photo, 1961-62.
Sam Daniluk: portable typewriter "Hermes baby
  featherweight" & cleaning supplies, 1945.
Mrs. M.M. Dunn: newspapers, articles & clippings about
  the Azalea Festival & local historic sites, 1960s.
Evelyn R. Foster: postcards: Carolina Apts., 1909; Odd
  Fellows Temple, 1911; Lumina, 1912.
Douglas A. Fox: postcards of historic Wilmington,
  Wrightsville & Carolina beaches, 1940-50.
Jack F. Hart, Jr.: hammer & hatchet from construction of
  Dow Chemical plant, 1933.

Lillian Kersh: boating & water safety manuals,
  1975-1986.
Edna Williams Mason: James Walker Hospital nurse's
  uniform, 1950-51.
Norman H. Melton: fossils from horse, crocodile &
  buffalo of the Lower Cape Fear.
Ann S. Mincy: rifle & bayonet, Japanese Army, 1945;
  tools used by T.N. Simmons.
Wanda Moore: photo of Robert Moore, ca. 1975.
NC Azalea Festival: posters, 1992 & 1995.
Glenn Tetterton Opheim: dish towel from Tickhill
  Estfeld Primary School, Doncaster, England, 1995.
Charlotte J. Parker: programs, magazines & ID pins,
  1989-93.
Marilyn Pierce: USAF memorabilia from Leon Pierce,
  1941-53; newspaper articles about regional history.
E. L. "Buck" Potter: Stevens .22 caliber rifle, c. 1930;
  Winchester .32-.40 caliber rifle, c. 1900.
Robert L. Pratt: camera collection, 1899-1962.
Jimmy Savage: men's cologne ampules, 1960s.
Lydia McK. Stokes: US Army tunic, jodhpurs & Sam
  Browne belt, 1930s.
Doug Swink: Lumina ad, 5/20/46.
Helen Willetts: *Coast/Vacationer's Guide* & Bald Head
  Island license plate, 1975.
A. Jarvis Wood, Jr.: *The Health Bulletin*, Oct. 1954.
Frances D. Worrell: professional floor model hair dryer,
  c. 1940.
E.B. & Della W. York: cast-iron cooking/wash pot;
  unearthed near Currie, NC, 1950.

Image Archives

Robert Cantwell: videotape of Wilmington waterfront
  fire, 1953.
Barry Faulkner: photos of Hurricane Hazel damage to
  Carolina Beach, 1954.
Mary M. Gornto: photo of 8 Wilmington businessmen,
  including W.H. & Alex Sprunt, Thomas R. Orrell in
  Paris, 1922.
Wayne Jackson: WMFD-TV photos & log sheet for first-
  day broadcast, c. 1954.
Michelle Matheny: photo of Michael Jordan in
  Birmingham Barons uniform, 1994.
Mrs. Leslie Silva: photos of Nelson Silva & his Simmons
  Sea-Skiff, 1987 & 1993.
Annie Talley: photos of 1955 Sea-Skiff.
Kenneth L. Todd: photo of Michael Jordan & Jarrad
  Taunt, 1982.
Thomas E. Williams, Sr.: photo of Laney HS basketball
  team w/ Michael Jordan, 1980-81.

Unaccessioned Donations

Jay Barnes: book: *North Carolina's Hurricane History*,
  1995.
Nancy Faye Craig: magazines: *American Home*, Mar. &
  Aug. 1961; *Better Homes & Gardens*, Dec. 1956.
Betty J.B. Deangury: *1938 National Guard of the United
  States, State of NC* yearbook .
Ray Dew: loblolly pine cookies (cross-section), 1995.
Jack F. Hart, Jr.: photo of Dow Chemical employees
  near highway historical marker, 1993.
Jack Miller: 5 issues of New York *Times*, 1918-1919.
Susan Morgan: baby's lace jacket; lace & embroidery
  slip, c. 1910.
Jessie Moseley: nightgown & scarf, c. 1950; book, *Blue
  Book Speller*, c. 1920.
NC Azalea Festival: Azalea Festival posters,
  1992 & 1995.
NC Wildlife Commission: flying squirrel.
NHC Public Library: books: *Indian Wars in North
  Carolina*, 1963; *Printing in North Carolina*, 1946.
Julian Tusch: photocopy of newspaper article, "The All
  New Hanover County Basketball Team", 1981.
USDA: adult female beaver; 2 sub-adult male beavers.

Figure 4: An Acknowledgment Page from a Newsletter. This page acknowledges three different kinds of gifts: accessions, archives, and properties. This leaves no doubt as to the status of the gift. Courtesy of the Cape Fear Museum, *Waves and Currents*, 15, 2 (1995).

publication of a donor's name to legitimate museum functions such as exhibits or publication of catalogues.

Board Action

The board of trustees has the ultimate responsibility for the museum. When the museum accepts an object for its collection it is also accepting a rather heavy long-term responsibility and that makes it a board matter. The board should have knowledge, if not the actual approval, of the acceptance of each object. That does not necessarily mean that every object has to be taken before the board and discussed. That would tie the board up with minutiae that are best left to the professional staff. The easy way is to have the director take a list of accessions before the collections committee. Once approved, this can be submitted with the committee's report. By accepting the report the board approves of the accession. This action will give the board necessary oversight without creating undue interference.

On accepting a gift, it should be made clear to the donor that the museum does not expect any problems with acceptance; in fact, it is wise to mention, in passing, that the committee must approve. If the museum does not want the object this provision allows them to turn down the object gracefully, and spread the blame over the anonymity of a number of people. The acceptance of the collections report should be a routine thing, similar to the secretary's reading of the minutes. The report keeps the board informed, gives them some oversight over the collection, and reminds them of their responsibility.[8]

Properties Are Not Collections

Properties are expendable portable physical assets of the museum, such as desks, chairs, vacuum cleaners, lawn mowers, etc. These are items that will eventually wear out and have to be discarded. Properties are more of a problem for an accountant than a curator. The museum should state in the collection policy that the properties are not collections and they should not be treated as such. This means that properties should not be accessioned and that collection items should not be used as properties.

Many museums use reproductions of objects in their exhibits or for education programs. These reproductions are properties and should not be treated as collections even though you may keep them separate from the other properties. Particularly, they should not be accessioned.

If a reproduction is made by a well-known craftsman, it may have a high aesthetic, monetary, or cultural value. These objects might best be in the collection. This is a quandary, for if it is in the collection it should not be used in programs. We are going to discuss a tiered collection, where each tier receives different treatment, and that is one solution to the problem of valuable properties, if the museum can monitor it.

The Accession File

At this point you have a group of documents associated with the collection. These should be assembled into an accession file. Some museums have a separate file folder on each accession, some have a file on each object, and some have one for the year. The kind you use will depends on the number of documents you have and your ability to store them. In any case, the accession number should be written in soft (#2) pencil on each document, if it does not appear as part of the document itself, so that it is associated with the object. An accession file will continue to grow as letters and other documents come in, years after the file is set up. This is the permanent record of the museum and should be in a fire-resistant file cabinet, if you can afford one. It is not a bad idea to microfilm the accessions file periodically, and keep the film in a safe place.

What Not to Do and When Not to Do It

I repeat myself here about several things that I have already recommended that should not be done when acquiring an object. Once more, with feeling:

- Do not accept a gift without a transfer of title or buy an object without a bill of sale.
- Be very careful about accepting a gift that has any restrictions on it.

A major mistake a museum can make in the acquisition process is to put a valuation on the object for tax purposes. It is considered unethical to "buy" a donation with a high or inflated evaluation. It is illegal, too.[9] The museum can protect itself by making it part of the collection policy or registrar's manual not to make evaluations. *It is the donor's responsibility to get a correct value for the gift for tax purposes.* You should be more than willing to cooperate with the donor on getting a professional evaluation and by making the object available to the appraiser if necessary. As part of the gift, the donor may want the museum to pay the appraiser. This is the same, actually, as the museum making the appraisal, and it should not be done. You may lose an occasional object by refusing to do this, but you will keep your integrity.

On the other hand, value is often part of the description. You may have two china plates, one of them worth five hundred dollars and the other fifty cents. Another example would be an object associated with a famous person. The association gives it a value beyond its value as an artifact. An example might be a Civil War uniform. If worn by an anonymous soldier from an unknown locality it is a specimen. If worn by a local soldier whose history is known, then it is a valuable artifact. If you insure your collection you will usually have to place a value on each object in the collection. This is the "book" value. The book value should equal "fair market" value. The value should not be public information.

To Review

The first step in the registration process is the acquisition of the object. The museum must make sure that it actually acquires title to the object, that there are no restrictions on the museum's use of the object, and that all information about the object is recorded.

Notes

1. There is an extensive discussion of the acquisition process in Malaro, *Primer*, 52ff, on the subject of ownership see particularly, 56–69; Franklin Feldman, Stephen E. Weil, and Susan D. Biederman, *Art Law: Rights and Liabilities of Creators and Collectors*, 2 vols. (Boston: Little, Brown & Co., 1986), II, 1ff; Marilyn Phelan, *Museum Law: A Guide for Officers, Directors, and Counsel* (Evanston, IL: Kalos Kapp Press, 1994), 273–306. Stephen L. Williams, "Critical Concepts Concerning Non-Living Collections," *Collections* 1 (2004), 37–66, see especially "Accessioning," pp. 43–45 and "Cataloging," pp. 45–46. See also Clarissa Carwell and Rebecca Buck, "Acquisition and Accessioning," in Buck and Gilmore, *New Museum Registration Methods*, 157–166.

2. "Churning" consists of acquiring and disposing of objects rapidly.

3. Michael S. Shapiro, Brett L. Miler, Christine Steiner, and Nicholas D. Ward, ed., *Copyright in Museum Collections* (Washington, DC: American Association of Museums, 1999); John Awerdick and John Kettle III, "Copyright," in Buck and Gilmore, *New Museum Registration Methods*, 289–300; Malaro, *Primer*, 149–184; Malaro also discusses other rights that may, or may not, come with the object.

4. Timothy C. Keown, Amanda Murphy, and Jennifer Schansberg, "Ethical and Legal Issues: Complying with NAGPRA," in Buck and Gilmore, *New Museum Registration Methods*, 311–319.

5. Malaro, *Primer*, 56–59; Phelan, *Museum Law*, 94f.

6. Phalen, Museum Law, 99.

7. Malaro, *Primer*, 209. She also shows other forms mostly with much longer gift clauses.

8. Malaro, *Primer*, 13.

9. Phelan, *Museum Law*, 106, says that it is not illegal, under certain circumstances, for a museum to evaluate gifts, but then the museum becomes an interested party. Malaro, *Primer*, 25, says it is a bad practice and this view echoes the opinion of the museum field.

CHAPTER THREE

~

The Accession Number

Curators and registrars are fascinated by the accession number. They spend a great deal of time with the numbering system. Numbers are almost a mystical kind of thing but they are fairly simple when you look at them. The number system gives a unique identity to each object. That number is used to tie the records to the object. If your system assigns a unique number to each object, then you have cracked the first layer of the mysteries of numbering.[1]

The rule in developing number systems is the one used in computer programs—"KISS." Keep it simple stupid!

There are four kinds of numbers to consider:

- *Serial number*: This number is one in a series, usually beginning at one, and taking each number in sequence. Letters may be part of the system. All accession numbering systems in use today have a serial number as part of the accession number. Compare the "single-number system" and the "two-number system" below. They both are serial numbers.
- *Part number*: In this application, the number tells you something about the object as well as registering it with a unique number. The "three-number system" and its variations are part numbers but they are serial numbers as well.
- *Classification number*: This number is a kind of part number that indicates that the object belongs to a certain class of objects. Libraries use

them but a museum accession is usually not a book. Classification numbers work very well in libraries but not in museums. I do not recommend having a classification of the collection by number. I do not discuss them in this book.

- *Catalogue number*: Just what a catalogue number is, is rather vague. I have never had the need for it to be coherently explained to me. I will not discuss catalogue numbers in any detail in this book. I do not recommend having a catalogue number as a separate number from the accession number. The accession number can be considered a catalogue number. There is often confusion between what is a classification number and what is a catalogue number.[2]

The difference, if any, between an accession number and a registration number is discussed below. Let us look at how these different kinds of numbers are applied.

The Single-Number System

The easiest system to use is one with a single whole number for each object. The first object is numbered "1" (one), the second "2" (two), *seriatim*. The 912th object would be "912" and the 10,398th would be "10398." Nothing can be simpler than this! In fact, its logical construction and its very simplicity caused it to be used by the early museums in their first attempts to register objects. The Smithsonian Institution and National Park Service use a modified version of this system to this day. Although the single number system went out of style in the 1950s and has been replaced, the increasing use of computers for museum registration has caused some people to reevaluate this system.

A single-number system can be made to function as a part number if you pair it with another field, such as the name of the object. Using the name and the number together creates a part number. In fact, you will seldom, if ever, see the accession number listed alone, without any other field.

The single-number system has a lot going for it. The single-number system has no complications. It is easy to understand. One does not have to make decisions but simply take the next available number. This may be important in small museums with inexperienced or untrained staffs and, perhaps, periods with no staff. It also gives you the finite size of the collection.

There are some problems with the single-number system. If you get three accessions at once, of which one has two objects, one has eight, and the third has thirty-two, you have to complete the first accession before going on to the next. This is because your system is strictly sequential and does not easily allow for entering one object of an accession now and another later. If you tried to allow for this by assigning eight digits to the second accession and then went on to the third accession you would have a problem if you suddenly discovered nine objects, or only seven, in the second accession. The third accession of thirty-two objects may be much more important than the others, but you have to wait to do it until you have completed the other two because it is out of sequence. If the collection grows, the numbers may become very large. The donor of the objects is not identified in any particular way except as a block of numbers in a sequence. Museums account for their accessions by year but there is no particular way to identify accessions by year except, again, as a block of numbers.

The other problem is that, depending on how your data management system sorts numbers, you may have to put "leading zeros" on each number. These are discussed in detail below.

There is nothing wrong with the single-number system, but for the reasons listed above, the single-number system has fallen out of favor with museums and has been replaced by other systems that I will discuss below.

The Two-Number System

To resolve some of the problems with the single-number system, museums have adopted a number that I will call the control number. This control is usually the year the accession is made. If the year is 2008 then the control will be "008" for 2008. The second number is a catalogue number. The first item registered would be 008.1, the second 008.2, the 394th would be 008.394, etc. This system has some advantages. It divides the collections into blocks by year and makes accounting easier. It stops the incessant sequence of one number following another and allows you to deal with groups of objects.

Some museums write this number as XX.005. It is not too important which method you use as long as you are consistent. However, listing the year first makes a long string of numbers more readable. If there is a standard in the method of numbering it would be to list the year first.

The two-number system has solved the problem of always accessioning in the order received, but donors are not identified in any way by the numbering system.

The Three-Number System

Because of these considerations museums have developed what I will call the three-number system (sometimes called the "trinomial system"). In this system the second number is a source number and there is a third number that I will call the catalogue number. This number is added to the two-number system.

In the three-number system, the first number, or control, is usually the year of accession, the second the source number, and the third the accession or catalogue number. In this example, 008.23.14, "008" represents the year the accession was made (2008); "23" represents the twenty-third accession made in this year; and the "14" represents the fourteenth object in that particular accession. That is, there were thirteen objects registered before this one in the same accession. All objects numbered 008.23.XX come from the same source at the same time.

This number may also be written
14.23.008   or   23.008.14

It strikes me that people that have systems using one of the last two examples are just trying to be different. The numbers in the last two examples will not line on a page as well as they will when the year is placed first. That may be the reason that most museums place the year first, the control second, and the catalogue number third.

The main advantages of the three-number system are, first, you do not have to worry about how many objects there are in each accession. The system can take care of any number. I once had over 3,100 objects in one accession. One does not have to take the accessions in sequential order, although you do have to complete them all before the end of the year.

The second advantage, and perhaps the most important, is that it identifies the donor or source of the accession by number. In fact, as we shall see, the three-number system can convey a lot of information depending on how it is structured.[2]

The three-number system resolves most of the problems that plague the other two numbering systems. This is the reason it has been almost universally adopted by history museums in the United States today.

These three systems have withstood the test of time and will fit any museum situation. There is no reason for you to reinvent the wheel and develop your own system when these are perfectly acceptable.[3]

Which System Should You Use?

It is very difficult to advise anyone on which system to use without actually seeing the museum, talking to the people involved, and looking at the rationale of the collection. I would suggest considering these factors in selecting the numbering system you should use.

- The single-number system will best fit a small volunteer-run museum with a small collection and no real potential for growth. The system is simple to understand and administer. You can grasp the whole system with a quick glance in the records. If the collection should grow, or circumstances should change, the numbering system can always be changed to one of the other systems.
- The two-number system will best fit a museum where the museum has a small collection or the accessions are infrequent and small in size. An example where this system would be useful is a museum of historical paintings that has 250 items in the collection and acquires only eight or ten objects in six or eight accessions each year.
- The three-number system should be used in all other situations. This system is flexible and fits a variety of circumstances that come up every year in an active museum collection. The three-number system is standard in the history museum field and is readily understandable to museum professionals.

Contrary to what some people believe, the two-number and three-number systems will easily fit into most computer programs and can be easily sorted.

Collection Numbers

The control number can convey a lot of information and does not always have to represent the year of acquisition. It can be used to correct an anomaly in the system, as a collection number, or it can indicate a change in collection practices.

It is very common in older museums to have separate and distinctly defined collections existing inside the museum collection. Sometimes there is a good reason to separate these collections if only in the registration system. Perhaps the museum was once two separate and distinct institutions that have merged. Perhaps one was a schoolhouse museum and the other a mansion. They each have collections that should be kept apart, at least on paper.

One can identify these collections by several means. A collection number is usually a prefix on an existing number. It might look like this:

M32	S32
M32.1	S32.1
M32.1.1	S32.1.1

or

1.32	2.32
1.32.1	2.32.1
1.32.1.1	2.32.1.1

In these examples the "M" or "1" stands for "mansion" and the "S" or "2" stands for "schoolhouse. With either of these systems you can easily tell an item from one collection from an item from another, but you must be careful to avoid confusing one number with another. The letter version is a little shorter and more understandable, and is favored for that reason.

The collection number does not have to be a prefix but can be indicated by the year or the control number. I list several examples below.

The reason for discussing a collection number at all in a book aimed at small museums is that it is very common to find complete collections of known provenance already existing in the museum collection which, for one reason or another, have to be kept distinct from the rest of the collection. A typical example is a museum that is the successor of a DAR (Daughters of the American Revolution) museum. There is a requirement that the DAR museum be kept distinct from the successor museum's collection, at least in the records.

Someone gave the museum a collection of stuffed birds in 1910, and a log house museum and its contents in 1933. The museum was given a defunct school system museum in 1956. They completely modernized their registration system in 1962. If you think I am exaggerating, I am describing a collection I once administered (with the exception of the log house) along with thirty years of bad record keeping.

It is better to assign a control number than a collection number. In this case, the year of accession is used as the control number. It would be an "artificial" year. All things considered, a control number is a collection number. Using the examples given above, you would assign a separate control number for each collection. If you found these numbers in your collection then you would know quite a bit about the object.

909.26.XX (from the DAR museum founded in 1909)

910.26.XX (from the bird collection given in 1910)

933.26.XX (from the log cabin museum given in 1933)

956.26.XX (from the defunct school system museum given in 1956)

961.26.XX (from the museum collection before the modern registration system, which was started in 1962, but which does not contain any of the known collections listed above)

[From here on in, one would use the year of accession for the year number.]

962.26.XX (from the modern museum registration system adopted in 1962)

This arrangement will work best with the two- or three-number system, which may be one reason for adopting one of these systems. A version of this system can be used with the single-number system, using controls with the earlier collections, and a single number with the new accessions.[4]

Using a Number to Indicate Special Conditions

Another use of special numbering techniques in a registration system is to indicate certain characteristics of the collection. If you have large numbers of objects that are "unknown" or "found in the collection," a special source number might be a way of indicating them. If you give all unknowns the accession number "1" (one) each year, then they will be readily apparent. A number such as 009.1.34 will tell you that this object is of unknown origin.

We used a system at Old Economy Village.[5] In 1965 the whole collection was of "unknown" origin. It had all been acquired in 1938 but only a partial registration of the collection had been made. There had been some unrecorded acquisitions later. We gave all unknowns the control number "1" with the exception of Harmony Society–related items, which were later given the control number "2." Examples would be

75.1.XX (object of unknown origin found in the collection),

75.2.XX (unknown object of presumed Harmony Society manufacture or use),

75.3.XX (an acquisition that was accessioned using normal practices), *seriatim*.

Accounting for unknowns in this fashion does not relieve you from eventually having to get good title to them.

Accession Ledgers

It was a common practice for museums in the eighteenth, nineteenth, and early twentieth centuries to have accession ledgers. These ledgers are usually bound record books in which the objects are usually listed in the order of acquisition. These ledgers were a combination of register and accession record. The ledgers often contain the name of the object, a brief description, and the name of the donor or source. There is, more often than not, a number assigned to each object. These accession ledgers, if well kept, were considered quite adequate for the time, and can be the basis of a good registration system even today. There are large modern museums that are presently still using a form of accession ledger and doing quite well. I am going to recommend using a version of it in the bound accession records. You have to recognize that an electronic file in a computer is a form of ledger.

In the case where no number is assigned to the object in the ledger, you should make a working copy of the ledger and number the objects sequentially beginning at the front of the book. As you find objects you can put the number that belongs on the object. The two- and three-number systems work best in these cases. If a number has been assigned in the ledger, use that number. If there are inconsistencies you will have to work them out. Be sure not to use the original book, as it is a primary record. Make a copy.

Registers, especially those used to track accession numbers, and ledgers, are discussed in the next chapter.

How to Handle the Centuries

If the museum's collection predates the twenty-first century, there must be a way to tell one century apart from another. The most common way to handle this is to assign the whole year to the accession number:

1786.32.3	1886.32.3	1986.32.3	2086.32.3

or

786.32.3	886.32.3	986.32.3	086.32.3

With this system you can easily tell in which century the object was accessioned. A single-number system does not require any adjustment for centuries.

Letters

A certain condition will come up before you get very far into the registering the collection. What do you do about pairs and sets. These are such things as a pair of shoes or stockings, a cup and saucer, a pair of andirons, a set of dishes, a chess set, etc. It is a common practice to number small sets or suites with letters. This practice of using letters to indicate a set is applied mainly to objects that will normally be always associated with each other and where there are only two or three pieces in the set, such as gloves and stockings. If you have a set of dishes with 153 pieces letters will not work.

In sets of objects, such as dining room chairs, you should number each object individually. Although strongly associated with each other, the chairs will not always be kept together. It is confusing to give all the chairs the same number and then label each one separately "A," "B," etc.

A common practice in collections is to do something like this:

988.12.2A   Teapot
988.12.2B   Lid

Notice I use capital letters. When the accession number is written on the object, capital letters are less easily confused with numbers than lowercase letters. A *b*, *a*, or *d* can look like a 6, and an *f* like a 5 or *2*, etc.

Sometimes you see numbers used instead of letters:

988.12.2.1   Teapot
988.12.2.2   Lid

I do not recommend the latter system.

When to use letters or not is something you are going to have to spend some time thinking about. It gets awkward if you number more than four or five objects with letters. It gets practically impossible when you reach the twenty-seventh object and run out of letters (though I have seen the use of double letters such as 004.27AA). That means you use letters on such things as pairs of candlesticks, but use numbers on a set of dining room chairs. What your policy is should be part of your collection practices manual.[6]

Loan Numbers

The necessity for loan numbers is discussed in chapter 7. It is important that whatever system of numbering loans you use that you do not confuse your loan numbers with your accession numbers. It is a common practice to reverse the accession number to get a loan number, thus

Accession number   Loan Number
986.23.2   2.23.986

With this system, however, you will inevitably get the two numbers confused at some point of time. The best method is to place the letter "L" (for "loan") in front of the loan number and change the order you list the numbers:

Accession Number   Loan Number
86.23.2   L2.23.86

In the example the "L2.23.86" is the second object in the twenty-third loan in the year 1986. There will be less likelihood of confusion using this method. An example of a ledger for loan numbers is shown in the appendix.

The Difference between an Accession, Registration, Catalogue, and Classification Number

Some people place a great deal of significance on the number and almost treat it as a mystical thing. The only purpose of the number is to give you a handy method of identifying the object. It's handier than using letters or writing the data on the object itself.

There is a number used to tie the object to the records. That number is created and placed on the object when the object is accessioned. That is why the numbers are usually called "accession numbers." When the object is accessioned it has been registered. So this same accession number is also a registration number. Why some museums have two numbers for this purpose has completely escaped my comprehension.

Objects are usually classified in history museums by how the object is used. Since the number only ties the object to the record it cannot properly be called a classification number. Some museums create classification numbers. Classification numbers do not work well in a history museum. For a discussion of this, see particularly the section on lexicons in chapter 6.

The reason for having a catalogue number versus an accession number is so the number will classify or identify the object for you by the number alone. It is understandable that you might want to classify all the objects in the museum collection by their number. All the clothing would have one number, all the dresses would have a sub-classification under this, and a particular style of dress would have a sub-sub-classification, and so on. This has been attempted many times with varying degrees of success. As a matter of fact, you sometimes see collections catalogued with a system in which all tools begin with "T" and all the furniture begins with "F," etc. There are frequently sub-classifications such as "TC" standing for carpenters tools. These systems break down almost as soon as they are created.

A term such as "plane, smoothing" shows you exactly where to place the record in the catalogue. Calling a smoothing plane a "TC6" unnecessarily complicates the registration process, ignores the fact that you already have a perfectly good classification system by terminology, and is redundant besides.

Despite this, some museums have two numbers for each object; an accession number and a catalogue number. I have never understood why. The largest and best-run museums in the country have enough trouble keeping track of one set of numbers, let alone two, and you are no exception to this.

Many people look at a library catalogue and wonder why the same kind of numbering system will not work in a museum. A library classifies a book by its subject, and arranges the book alphabetically by author inside that classification. The difference between our system and the ones libraries use, is that the library number, in most cases, indicates where the book is shelved, something that will not work in a museum.

Actually we use a similar system based on what the object is called, but without the classification number, since the museum classification has nothing to do with where the object is stored. Some people in the museum field see the library classification number and think it would be perfect if a similar number would do their classification for them. There are a few systems out there that attempt this. I have seen a collection accessioned with Dewey decimal numbers, and it was not badly done, but normally such systems do not work. The museum catalogue is just a device to hold the catalogued list. Our catalogues are classified by broad families of objects with similar uses, and arranged by specific uses inside that. Individual objects are classified by what they are called. An accession number is not a classification number, but just a device to identify a particular object. It is more on the order of a part number.[7]

Numbers and Computers

A computer can process almost any kind of accession number, and, better yet, handle several different numbering systems at once.

However, the numbering system used in a museum and the computer come frequently into conflict. The problem is not in the entry; it is in the computer. You can create a field that will take anything you can create on a keyboard. The problem is to get this to sort in some logical sequence. More and more, computer programs will logically sort accession numbers, but this is not always true. There is a solution for those that won't.

If you have a six figured field (xxxxxx) and put a number in the first field (1xxxxx), many computer programs treat this as the number 100,000 not 1 (one). Letters often do not always sort in any logical sequence as the lower case "a" may come after 9 (nine) and uppercase letters sometimes sort differently than lowercase, etc. This would not be a problem so much except that the periods, in a number such as 993.87.62, cause the accession number to be sorted as if it were letters.

There are several ways around this. The best method is to look for a program that will handle your numbering system(s). If you cannot find that, the most common solution is to fill the blanks with zeros, called "leading zeros." The number 1 (one) will look like this:

000001

Keep in mind that it is better that the leading zeros are used only in the accession record and not on the object.

In new registration systems you can avoid the need for leading zeros by starting your sequence with a higher number. If you have fifteen thousand objects you start the series with ten thousand. That is, the first number in the accession register will be 10001 instead of 00001. In my example, you will have room for 89,999—most often more than enough.

You can put each element of the number in a separate field but this only puts the problem into several places instead of one.

More and more computer programs are designed to get around this problem. It is one of the questions you should ask about when buying a program.

Numbering Digital Images

Digital images have a problem in that the camera may arbitrarily assign a file number to each image. You can easily lose control of the image number when this happens. The ideal system is to use accession number as the image number. You can save the image by accession number to get around this problem. You should make the accession number part of the image by including it with the image. Mark the number on a card and photograph it along with the image of the object.

Other Types of Numbering Systems

The numbering systems I have described work best with a history museum collection. There are other numbering systems for books, archives, and archaeological specimens. Science museums have several methods that fit their varied collections. When assigning numbers to these specialized collections it is best to use the system common to the discipline. However, if you have a small collection of such objects, it may not pay to set up a separate numbering system for just a few objects. As an example, at Old Economy we accessioned books that were part of the collection, using a standard museum system, and used the Library of Congress system on the reference books.

Conclusion

When beginning or updating a registration system it is important to spend a little time developing the numbering system that suits your situation. The system can make it a lot easier on you later. There is nothing particularly complicated about numbering systems. If they are well thought out they tend to maintain themselves, once they are in place. They can affect the ease of entering data and accessioning. It is wise to set up a system that fits your needs rather then adopt someone else's system. There is nothing to stop you from adopting a new numbering system as your needs change, although I would caution you against renumbering the whole collection.

Notes

1. Buck and Gilmore, *New Museum Registration Methods*, 43–44.

2. An example of a registration system using catalogue numbers can be seen in the system used by the National Park Service. The park service uses a single-number system for its accession number and another single-number system for its catalogue number, which must cause endless confusion when these two sets of numbers inevitably equal each other. They have taken some steps to solve this problem. Buck and Gilmore, *New Museum Registration Methods*, contains the word "catalogue" only for cards or sheets.

3. A number of my friends feel the three-number system was developed to account for the source of the object, but I feel it was developed to resolve the problems of the other two systems. The problems with the single-number and two-number system

would not be as great if you were using only a ledger, but the three-number system works better with cards.

4. A good example of the need for a collection number can be seen in the Pennsylvania Historical and Museum Commission. The PHMC has about sixty separate historic sites and museums, some of which have collections that are made distinct by law. The PHMC assigns a two-letter code to each site or museum (Old Economy is "OE" and the number would be OE67.23.9). A master number was kept by the registrar, but this did not appear on the object. A well-designed computer program can obviate the need for collection numbers.

5. Old Economy Village is a historic-site museum in Ambridge, Pennsylvania, founded by the Harmony Society in 1824 and administered by the Pennsylvania Historical and Museum Commission.

6. Sue Hanna, then collections manager of the Pennsylvania Historical and Museum Commission, argued during a presentation on cataloguing at the 1992 MAAM Annual Meeting that if all parts of the object have letters then one could tell there was more than one part to the object should the parts be separated.

7. Buck and Gilmore, *New Museum Registration Methods*, has a brief discussion of numbers, 43–44.

CHAPTER FOUR

⌒

Accessioning

Accessioning: A formal process used to accept legally and to record a specimen or artifact as a collection item (Malero, 1998); involves the creation of an immediate, brief, and permanent record utilizing a control number or unique identifier for objects added to the collection from the same source at the same time, for which the museum accepts custody, right, or title.[1]

The second stage of registration is the accessioning process. To accession an object means to take it into the museum's collection. This is a serious step.

Before the object is accessioned it is a piece of property with which the owners can do anything they wish: they can give it to their Uncle Charley, destroy it, paint it green, or put it out in the barn. A property (such as a vacuum cleaner) is a depreciable item whose life is measured by the accounting practices of the museum. Property will eventually be disposed of with very few regrets or complications.

An accession is a different matter. Once an object is accessioned into a museum collection it takes on a whole new life. It becomes something that is protected by law and custom. An accessioned object is meant to be given highly specialized care and kept forever. Disposing if it, called deaccessioning, is a complicated process that takes considerable amount of time and effort and may result in an adverse public controversy.[2]

It is wise therefore to have a well-thought-out accession policy that is strictly applied. The reason for having a sound accession policy is that means you have fewer chances of accessioning objects that you will later have to deaccession. You must have a sound deaccession policy as well.

The accessioning process consists of making a place for the object in the museum registration system and creating a permanent record of it. The accessioning process consists of the following steps:

1. Acquiring right and title to the object. I have discussed this process in chapter 2 on acquisition.
2. Assigning an accession number. I have discussed this in chapter 3 on numbers.
3. Making a record of the object.
4. Marking the object.

These actions are usually done all at once, but each is a separate process. It is important that the object be accessioned almost immediately after the museum takes possession of it or some of the information that comes with it will be lost.

Creating a Record for the Object

Each object must have a primary record of its existence. This is usually called the "accession record." It is created from a worksheet or a screen in the electronic record. Each of these individual records should be distinct from all the others. It should follow a format so that the same types of information are recorded for each object, and that the information is adequate. You can have many problems if you assign more than one accession to a record, have gaps in the sequence, misnumber the object, or do not record enough information. I am not going into all the problems, but almost all difficulties with records start with poor accession practices.

The Log

Since the number identifies each accession you must have a method of assigning accession numbers in some logical sequence that will assure that there are no gaps or duplicates. A simple way to control this is to have a log. A log need only be a simple stenographer's notebook where each accession is listed with its accession number in the order assigned. These are checked off as the records are created. At the end of the year the whole log is checked off against the ledger to make sure that all accessions are recorded.

```
93.1.1    BOOK   LIVES OF SIGNERS
93.1.2    DECORATIVE  TILE
93.1.3    PENCIL SKETCH OF PAPER MILL
93.1.4    POSTCARD  FOLDER
93.1.5    LITHOGRAPH , LADY W's RECEPTION
93.1.6    LITHOGRAPH , B. ROSS
93.1.7    ENGRAVING , LORD STIRLING
93.1.8    INDENTURE    OBA/STATE NJ
93.1.9    ENGRAVING    WM. PENN
93.1.10   RUG
93.1.11   WARMER, FOOT
93.1.12   BOX, CONTRIBUTION
93.1.13   FLAG      BICENT OF INAUG.
93.1.14   "|         "|   "|   "|
93.1.15   "|         "|   "|   "|
93.1.16   POSTCARD   NY WORLD's FAIR 1938
93.1.17   PAMPHLET   "| "|   "|   "|
93.1.18   PHOTOGRAPH OB
93.1.19   "|          "|
93.1.20   "|          "|
93.1.21   "|          "|
93.1.22   COVERLET - ANN DOUGLASS
93.1.23   PHOTO    WWI RED CROSS
```

Figure 5:   Log. The log is a handy way to track objects in the accessioning process. The accession is entered when it arrives at the museum. As soon as it is entered in the ledger or data bank, the log entry is marked off.

A log helps the lone professional, who has many distractions, keep track of the accessions. A log is very useful in a museum that has a number of people accessioning objects. It gives the registrar control over the issuing of numbers. A log is useful with either a computer or manual system. It is one of those low-tech things in our hi-tech world that is so useful in keeping everything on the right track. (See figure 5.)

The Register

The log is not a permanent record. You need some permanent and unalterable way of recording the sequence. The device you use is a register. This register can be created in a number of ways. (See figure 6.)

Manual Systems

With a manual system the register should be in a bound record book that keeps the whole list of accessions for the museum in the proper sequence. You can have a separate register, or use a ledger, which I will discuss below, in its place. With paper records I prefer to keep a separate accession register, but if you can keep good control over the ledger, a separate register is not necessary.

The purpose of the register is to keep your accessions in order so it need not carry much information. All that is necessary is the accession number, a brief description of the accession, the source, and the date. Entry into the register should be made at the time the accession is recorded. If you let it go, you may find it difficult to complete the entries accurately later. The register acts as a catalogue of all the accessions stored by number.[3]

Computer Systems

A computer system can generate its own register. You will still need some sort of log to make sure that the number you assign is in some sort of succession with all the other numbers and there are no gaps or duplicates.

The Worksheet

There has to be a way to capture the information on the object and put it in your records. At one time this would have been a worksheet. This worksheet contained all the fields you needed to capture for a complete record. The paper worksheet has mostly been replaced by a screen in the computer program. Some museums still use the paper worksheet, which is filled in by an expert and used by a less-experienced person to enter the data electronically. This

Acc. Number	Object Name	L	S	C	P	FLG	Material	Date	Value	Location	Source L N
056.002.001.	Plaque	y	g	c	4		Wax	1810	$1200	C	Atterbury Es
056.002.006.	Mezzotint	y	g	c	5		Paper	1798	$500	B	Atterbury Es
056.002.00b.	Gun, Market	y	g	d	3		Steel; Walnut	1820	$2000	A08/09/10a	Atterbury Es
056.002.00c.	Sundial	y	d			99	Bronze	1750		Deacc	Atterbury Es
056.002.00d.	Engraving	y	d			99	Paper	1823		Deacc	Atterbury Es
056.002.00e.001	Photograph	y	g	c	5		Paper	1920	$10	Ephemera 1	Atterbury Es
056.002.00e.002	Sketch, Ink	y	g	c	3		Paper	1880	$250	Ephemera 1	Atterbury Es
056.002.00g.	Painting, Oil	y	g	c	4		Oil; Canvas	1760	$5000	D	Atterbury Es
056.002.00h.	Engraving	y	g	e	2		Paper	1840	$10	Map1-3	Atterbury Es
056.002.00i.001	Engraving	y	g	c	5		Paper	1891	$500	A13a 028	Atterbury Es
056.002.00i.002	Letter	n	g	c	3		Paper	1864	$1000	Ephemera 1	Atterbury Es
056.002.00j.	Broadside	y	g	c	4		Paper	1778	$96	B	Atterbury Es
056.002.00k.	Settee	y	d			99		1800		Deacc	Atterbury Es
056.002.001.	Engraving	y	g	d	3		Paper	1850	$100	Map1-3	Atterbury Es
056.002.00m.	Waistcoat	y	g	c	4		Silk; Linen; Cotton	1780	$520	Ai2b 032	Atterbury Es
056.002.00n.	Table, Side	y	d			99	Walnut	1800		Deacc	Atterbury Es
056.002.00o.	Chair	y	g	c	5		Mahogany	1790	$4500	D	Atterbury Es
056.002.00p.	Waist (dress?)	y	d			99				Deacc	Atterbury Es
056.003.00a.	Ledger	y	g	c	3		Paper	1766	$100	A15	Pidcock
056.003.00b.	Ledger	y	g	c	4		Paper	1872	$100	A15	Pidcock
056.005.000.	Secretary	y	d			99				Deacc	OBA
056.006.001.	Sleeve	y	?	c	5		Silk	1880	$10	A12c 016	Unknown
056.006.002.	Sleeve	y	?	c	5		Silk	1880	$10	A12c 016	Unknown
056.007.001.	Ring, Hair	y	?	d	3		Hair; Silk	1805	$10	Ephemera 1	Hughes
056.007.002.	Letter	y	g	c	4		Paper	1890	$1	Ephemera 1	Hughes
056.010.000.	Rug	n	f	c	4		Wool		$100	A20f A203	Found in Col
057.001.000.	Painting, Oil	y	g	c	5		Oil; Canvas	1825	$6080	D	McKesson
057.002.000.	Painting, Oil	y	g	c	5		Oil; Canvas		$5920	D	McKesson
057.002.00n.	Act	n	f	c	4		Paper	1811	$10	Ephemera 1	Found in Col
057.003.000.	Quilt Fragment	y	g	c	4		Cotton; Silk	1860	$25	A12b 018	Arnold
057.004.004.	Plate, Serving	y	g	b	5		Glass		$43	A07b	Case
057.004.006.	Plate, Dinner	y	g	d	4		Earthenware		$50	A07b	Case
057.004.00a.	Quilt	y	g	c	5		Silk; Cotton	1845	$5120	A12a 013	Case
057.004.00b.	Sampler	y	g	c	5		Silk; Linen	1819	$1500	B	Case
057.004.00c.	Rug	y	g	c	3		Wool		$200	A20c A216	Case
057.004.00e.	Spoon, Serving	y	g	b	5	VA	Silver		$156	Vault 001	Case
057.005.000.	Platter	y	g	c	5		Porcelain(?)	1790	$500	A01c	Rickert
057.006.000.	Plate	y	g	c	4		Earthenware	1750	$150	A07b	Hutchinson
057.007.001.	Candlestick	y	g	c	5		Glass	1835	$150	A13e	Biles Est.
057.007.002.	Candlestick	y	g	c	5		Glass	1835	$150	A13e	Biles Est.
057.008.001.	Jug, Toby	y	g	b	5		Earthenware	1940	$1000	A07e	van Syckel
057.008.002.	Jug, Toby	y	g	b	5		Earthenware	1940	$1000	A07e	van Syckel
057.008.003.	Jug, Toby	y	g	b	5		Earthenware		$2000	A06e	van Syckel
057.008.004.	Jug, Toby	y	g	c	4		Earthenware	1795	$1000	A06e	van Syckel
057.008.005.	Cellar, Salt	y	g	c	5		Earthenware	1880	$50	A07e	van Syckel
057.008.006.	Shaker, Pepper	y	g	c	5		Earthenware	1880	$50	A07e	van Syckel
057.008.007.	Jug, Toby	y	g	c	5		Earthenware	1868	$500	A07f	van Syckel
057.008.008.	Cruet	y	g	c	5		Earthenware	1880	$50	A07e	van Syckel

Figure 6:   Register. The register keeps track of the accession number. The example is generated by a computer, which is much easier than generating a list from a manual register. The computer-generated register is also handy in making inventories and handling large blocks of data. Courtesy of the Old Economy Museum.

Hero County Historical Society
WORKSHEET

Accession Number:
Old Number:

Title of Object:

Classification:

How acquired: Source:

Location:

Material: Flag:

Size: Value:

Place of origin:

Maker:

Date (of manufacture):

Description: Image no.

Association:

Comment:

Compiler:

Figure 7:   Worksheet. The worksheet captures all the information you need to accession the object. You should arrange the fields in the order you enter them in the ledger
or data bank. The fields selected for this example are the ones suggested in chapter 8
on computers. I have placed a box to receive digital images. You should have some provision to enter more than one image in the record. If you do not track certain data, such
as value, you need not include it. This same sheet can act as a permanent accession
record. You can get a record like this on one screen.

is a viable alternative if you do not have a computer in every work area. (See
figure 7.)

The Ledger

The ledger is all the accession information gathered into one place. The old
museum ledgers were bound books. If complete and accurate these bound

ledgers were excellent devices that kept all the museum registration information in one place. It might be almost impossible to easily extract information from them, but they did store the records better than any other system, even a computer. Some museums use them to this day, in many cases generating them by a computer. I am strongly recommending that you have some type of accession ledger whether paper or digital. Your worksheet is a good model for a ledger page.

Manual Systems

There are several methods of creating a ledger manually. The easiest way is to type up your accession sheets and bind these periodically, say once a year. This method has the advantage that the technology is simple and cheap.

An older technology is to write the ledger information in a bound book. This may sound dreadfully old fashioned, but for very small museums this method might be a very viable alternative. Use India or an indelible ink on good paper. An example of a typed ledger page is shown in the appendix.

It is not a good idea to place all the accession sheets in a file and call that a ledger. Loose files are easily disturbed, records lost, and the whole file misplaced. One of the reasons I recommend a bound book is the ability of these books to survive almost any disaster.[4]

It is possible to type your accession sheets in a word processor and create the ledger from that file. This is not a good practice. It strikes me that it is about as easy to type the records into a database and then you can do many more things with them that you cannot do with a word processor.

Computer-Generated Ledger

Generating a ledger entry from a computer data bank is a relatively easy process with almost any program with which I am familiar. (See figure 8.)

Whether it is practical to print all your data out or not is another matter. If you have ten thousand objects the ledger may very well be ten thousand pages long. Bound at 250 pages per book this is forty volumes. As the ultimate backup this may be a very useful project, but it is a big project that may not be too practical. Since computer files are constantly updated this printed ledger can be considered a picture of the collection at one point in time. But what if you have fifteen thousand objects (sixty volumes), or twenty-five thousand objects (one hundred volumes)? There are computer service companies who will be able to print this out for you. They are widely available and you can find them in the yellow pages. An electronic backup may be a more practical solution. The ledger can be written to the screen very easily. Computers are discussed in chapter 8.

Acc. Number	Object Name	Description	Comments	Source L Name
056.002.001.	Plaque	George Washington; faces viewer's right; profile head and shoulders; in military uniform; hair in que; set against dark chipped crystal ground; oval shadow box with frame of gilded wood; ball molding around edge; On back is typed label, "This bas-relief of Washington formerly belonged to Dr. Elias Boudinot of Burlington, N.J., and was bequeathed by him to Lewis Atterbury, husband of Catherine, daughter of his [Boudinet's] brother, Elisha Boudinet. Lewis Atterbury gave it to his son, Edward J.C. Atterbury of Trenton, N.J., and he to his son Albert H. Atterbury of Plainfield, N.J. Elias Boudinet's will is recorded in the Prerogative Court of New Jersey at Trenton: The seventeenth paragraph reads: "I give my nephew, Lewis Atterbury, the bust of General Washington taken in white wax."	Artist is an attribution, but a good possibility;2/81, 1/8" crack at base of neck in front, becoming hairline halfway across; 1/93,cracked at neck; frame cracked in several places; originally belonged to Elias Boudinot, Burlington; list of owners on back;	Atterbury Est.
056.002.006.	Mezzotint	George Washington;head and shoulders; shoulders turned to viewer's left and head front; "Geo. Washington Esqr. Late president of the United States of America'; "From an original picture in the possession of J. Seb De Franca Esqr of Devonshire Place to whom this plate is dedicated by . . . Robt. Cribb. [publisher]"; signed "C.G. Stuart pinxt" lower left and W. Nutter sculpt" lower right; "London Published Jany 15 1798 by Robert Cribb Holborn; framed; glass painted black with gold trim to resemble mat;	4/81 print glued to cardboard; removed from frame by Jack Koeppel; 7/93, foxed;	Atterbury Est.
056.002.00b.	Gun, Market	Probably a Spanish wall gun, as it has trunions, and later used as a market gun; muzzle loader; percussion, but has an unusual cap and hidden nipple; trigger is a button; full stocked with	Used by Anthony A. Livingston, grandfather of donor; stock broken in move of 1996.	Atterbury Est.

Figure 8: **Computer-Generated Ledger. The ledger information is mostly gathered at the time the object is accessioned. The ledger in a manual system is the worksheet information gathered in a book form. In this example the ledger information is in a data bank and accessed from a screen. It may not be printed out at all, or only once for a paper file on the accession. Courtesy of the Old Barracks Museum.**

Remember this! Data stored in electronic form deteriorates over time, nor do the programs that read this data last indefinitely. The life of a program is typically about five years and companies often do not "support" them for even that length of time. Without the program you may not be able to read the data. Printed on good paper, the written record lasts almost forever. It may pay to print out your whole file once in a lifetime, even if you have a huge collection.

Capturing the Information

Some museums divide the accession information on the object into two separate categories of accession information and catalogue information. Whether this difference has any meaning to a small museum is a moot point, but all this information should be written down at the time the object is accessioned. This information is gathered on a worksheet.

Lately museums have been thinking about a system that will allow one to extract more information from the records than the name of the object. What the content of the record should be was taken up by the Common Agenda Data Bases Task Force in the late 1980s. This was the first real (and about the only) attempt to develop a system that had a standard definition of data fields common to all history museums.[5] Not much further work has been done on this concept since, but it was a worthwhile project, and very usable. I show a worksheet made up of the Common Agenda data fields below.

Accession Information
The accession information needed is relatively simple. One needs only

1. Name of the object
2. Source (name of donor or vendor)
3. Any restrictions or limit on the accession
4. Value (if the museum collects that information)
5. Size
6. Description
7. Date of acquisition
8. Location
9. An image if you are taking pictures

Catalogue Information
One acquires catalogue information by discussions with the source of the accession, by examination of the object itself, and through research. The Common

Agenda Data Bases Task Force separated catalogue information into descriptive data and historical data. Whatever you call it, the best time for you to capture it is at the time of the accession. See chapter 6 on cataloguing.

The reason for making a point about the difference between catalogue and accession data is that in some museums two different departments involving two different people might be responsible for collecting this data. The small museum seldom has to worry about this sort of thing.

As part of the capture of all the information associated with the object the museum should develop a record form that has a field for each discrete piece of information. A field is one particular piece of information such as the accession number, the name of the object, or the date of manufacture. I suggest some fields in the chapter on computers. The task force has divided the data into major groups of fields.

Management Data

This is, according to the task force's definition, "data normally recorded or created when an object comes into a collection, and data recorded as a means of relating objects and records to one another." This information is what some museums would call "accession" data.

Descriptive Data

The definition of this information is, "data that can be gathered about an object by observing it or by applying fairly simple research techniques, such as discovering an object's name or title." I like to think that this is information that the object itself tells you. This information is what some museums would call "catalogue" data.

Historical Data

Historical data is described as "data that provides a historical context for objects, relating them to people, organizations, places, events, and concepts." This is the data that is hardest to acquire but is the most important. I discuss historical data in chapter 5, "Documentation."

Descriptions

There is quite a difference between descriptive information written for a manual record and one for a computer. For paper records, compactness and succinctness is a plus. The information is concentrated rather than expanded. A computer may not be able to read a number of abbreviations or handle cryptic notes such as "somewhat like 22.8.6." The computer may well look on such things as a pair of andirons as one object, but with a paper record you can easily distinguish that there are two objects.

The information below is mainly for manual records although useful for both media. For a computer record some of the information, such as size, classification, name, provenance, etc., would go in separate fields. I discuss this in chapter 8, "Computers."

The basic part of the record of a properly registered object is the description. Descriptions should be simple and short, but complete enough to be used in court. If you follow the journalistic who, what, where, when, and why, you will have a fairly complete description. If you always describe objects using the same criteria in the same order you will not miss much and all your descriptions will be complete. If you set up a data table it makes things easier. A worksheet will do this for you. The computer essentially sets up a data table on-screen with all its separate fields such as below.

Nomenclature: Table, Dining

Classification: Category 2: Furniture

Provenance: New England, perhaps made in Zeus. In Jones family since before 1858. William Jones IV, donor.

Association: Jones family; donor says William Jones (I) wrote the town charter on table, ca. 1858

Date: 1810–1830

Description: Four inside-tapered legs; rectangular top; outside batten, flush drawer; brass mushroom pulls; stained and varnished

Material: walnut; poplar; brass

Condition: Excellent

Other information: Exhibited in NY Furniture Society exhibit "The New York Cabinetmaker," 1924; catalogue in acc. file. Hepplewhite style

Size: 64½"w × 38¾"d × 29½"h.

If written in a manual system as a description it might look like the sample below. In a computer the information would be in several different fields as shown above.

005.26.1 Table, dining: New England, early 19th century (1810–1830); perhaps local in manufacture; Jones family association; donor says that grandfather (William Jones, 1822–1908) wrote Zeus town charter on this table in ca. 1858; Hepplewhite style; four inside-tapered legs; rectangular top; outside batten; flush drawer with brass mushroom pulls; walnut; stained and varnished;

excellent condition; exhibited in the New York Furniture Society exhibit, "The New York Cabinetmaker, 1924;" see catalogue in accession file; see also probate of Adam Jones will in courthouse; 64½"w × 38¾"d × 29½"h.

Notice that I qualified several statements in this accession. I used the statement "donor says . . .". An oral tradition about 150 years old is suspect, but it has been in his family. The donor did not know the exact dates of his grandfather's life, but what information was available is given so that details can be checked later. When I did not know the exact date I used "ca." for "circa," which means "about."

It is a good idea to do the research on each object as it comes in, before the registration process is completed. The dates his grandfather lived and worked, the courthouse records on its construction, and construction techniques available at the time all should have been researched. The typical small museum may not have the time to do all this when the accession is made, but the bones of the research will be there, if captured in the first place, and will be available when needed later.

Usually, one develops a sort of laconic style, leaving out all unnecessary wording. If subjectless or verbless statements separated by semicolons are used, the descriptions are shorter. These descriptions do not have to have any literary merit; they just have to be complete enough to identify that particular object. The descriptions should evoke an accurate picture in the reader's mind, especially if he or she is unfamiliar with the object. Describe what is unique to the object. Short, succinct descriptions are best. The reader of the records has to bring some knowledge with her or him.

Because of the use of a computer, many museums have reduced the description to a few brief comments, or done away with it altogether. This is not a good practice. The first consideration is that the description offers you a way to distinguish new classes of objects. You may be able to extract such information as whether a certain class of table has flush drawers (versus lipped drawers), which may be significant when compared to other data. The computer offers you a method of making these comparisons quickly, although this can be done with much more difficulty in manual records.

The second consideration is that if the object is stolen you have to have a description good enough to distinguish that object from all others of its type. You would be surprised how difficult it is to describe to the police how your unique handmade apple peeler is different from all the other unique handmade apple peelers.

The final reason for a description is that it helps you identify the object. For one reason or another, you may have to find objects by their descriptions rather than number or location. Using the search engines of a computer program you can find all the objects with certain characteristics, such as outside battens.

If you adopt the policy that the condition of the object will be described as either *pristine, excellent, good, fair,* or *poor* (corresponding to the school marks of A, B, C, D, or E), you save some space. A good practice in manual records is to assume that all objects in the collection are in good ("C") condition unless indicated otherwise, and again you save time. On computer records it would be better to fill in the blank, as the computer will have difficulty differentiating a whether a blank means "C" or nothing.

Measure accurately. On large objects, measure to the sixteenth of an inch, and on small ones measure to the thiry-second. Some registrars have the practice of measuring to the next largest unit of measurement. That is, if you measure 3¾₆ inches you then record 3¼ inches That method has a lot to recommend it. Many museums use a metric system and measure to the millimeter. Some museums put both means of measurement in their records but that may be too much for the small museum. Adopt a policy of which system you will use so that one person does not use the inch/foot and the other the metric system. It is easy to configure most data management programs to convert one measurement to the other so that by entering an inch/foot measurement (for instance) you will automatically get the metric measurement.

It is best to take the overall outside measurements in particular order. If you measure the width first, then the depth and then the height it will help to ensure consistency and simplify your work when you prepare exhibits.

The museum often receives a number of objects that are more or less identical, such as a set of dinner plates. When you are using manual records it is best to take one object that is typical of all of them and describe it in detail. Then, for the rest, use the abbreviation *ibid.* which stands for *ibidem* and means "in the same place." *Ibidem* is a Latin word used in scholarly footnotes to refer to the citation before. Its use in the accession records refers only to the description immediately preceding it. If you have a dining room set with twelve matching side chairs, you pick the most typical chair and describe it, and then, for the others, you need only to mention minor variations following the word *ibid.* (Actually *idem*, abbreviated as *id.*, meaning "the same," would be more correct, but I am following the common practice.)

Even if the objects are not enough alike to use the term *ibid.*, it helps to line up similar objects. Then similar or unique characteristics will show up immediately. If you are accessioning a group of clothing items, place all the dresses in one pile, all the coats in another, and so on, instead of just grabbing items at random, as they come out of the trunk. (Although if the trunk is still the same order the way it was originally packed, that would be of interest.) You will be amazed at the way this simple method helps descriptions.

If you use a computer for cataloguing, the use of *ibid*. will not work. Computer searches will not know that it is to compare this record with the first in the series, at least in most programs. Even in the unlikely circumstance that the program can make such a search, it would be slower and more prone to errors than if you just have every object have its own description. However, the computer gives you the means to copy the first description to all the other records where it is needed.

Describe the usual characteristics and the unusual ones that mark the object. You would be surprised how often descriptions miss the obvious, such as the number of legs on a table. Some objects, such as stamps and coins, are described in catalogues. Referring to the catalogue number can simplify descriptions. Some classes of objects (such as carpenters planes) have a standard scholarly work written about them. Reference to the description in that work can save time. Do not make up words for technical descriptions. If you do not know what a ferrule is, call it a band of metal. Most technical terms come from only four sources, the parts of a human body, nature, mathematics, and architecture. If you learn the terminology for those four sources, you will be explicit even if you do not have the exact term. Clothing and decorative arts have a language all their own that must be learned eventually if you wish accurate descriptions. Consistency and accuracy are more important than a technical vocabulary.

The worksheet that I have mentioned before will ensure that you record all the data you need in the order you want it. A worksheet is useful when you are dealing with less-knowledgeable people or people in a training status. Even experienced curators will find worksheets useful. There is an example of a worksheet above and in the appendix. You will probably need a worksheet even if the information is stored in a computer. The worksheet does not have to be paper. It can be a screen on the computer.

Almost anything in the world can be described while standing on one foot. The second the other foot touches the ground, stop describing.

Marking Objects

Almost all the work you have done so far on registering an object will go to waste if you do not put the proper accession number on the object. The number ties the object to the records. Marking the object should be part of a definite chain of actions that you perform in the registration process. The process of accessioning should not be considered complete until the number is on the object.[6]

Marking the object is quite a complex process. You will end up with a different technique of marking for each type of object. The marking should not be visible when the object is displayed but should be easily found otherwise. The method of marking should not damage the object. The object should not be marked on finished surfaces. Finally, the number should be firmly attached to the object, so that it will last, but be easily removable if necessary.

Places such as inside the drawer on furniture, the bottom of plates, and the waistband of garments are all logical places to place a number on an object. On tools and implements there may be a problem in finding a hidden place for the number, as the tool may be viewed from any angle. Find as unobtrusive a place as possible. On large pieces, place the number where you will not have to move the piece to find it.

On objects that may occasionally be exposed to the weather, such as an automobile, or become greasy, such as a machine, the number has to be affixed in a very permanent manner. It might be a good idea to fasten a brass tag with wire onto such objects. It is a good idea to place marks on such pieces in several places. If you are consistent in marking one kind of object in the same place it will help those who follow after. After looking at a few of your accessions they will know where to look the next time the same kind of object comes up.

How you mark each object will vary from object to object. For objects with hard surfaces you may use India ink. Lay down a layer of acrylic and then put on the ink with a pen. You can find Speedball pens with small flat tips that will not scratch. India ink comes in several colors so it can contrast with any surface. That number will survive almost any treatment. It will even go through a dishwasher a couple of times. Yet it can be removed with a few swipes of nail polish remover.

I have used clear nail polish for almost forty years and found it works fine, but conservators are now very much opposed to its use. Conservators strongly recommend Soluvar (Acryloid B-67 + Acryloid F-10) or Acryloid B-72 (polyvinyl acetate). Any finish, or its solvent, used in the confines of a museum, has safety concerns. Make sure you read all instructions and warnings, and have good ventilation. Make sure that anything you use will not damage the surface of the object. It may be necessary to test before using the finish.

On dark surfaces many people place a strip of clear finish, then a strip of white acrylic paint. They write the number on the white with India ink and then apply another stripe of clear lacquer. Many museums prefer this method of marking to any other. White correction fluid comes in handy little bottles with brushes. Correction fluid will work, but poorly, and it often reacts with the lacquer you are using, so I do not recommend it. You can get white drawing ink that will save you a step in this situation.

A method that is used by one museum has something to recommend it. Print the accession number in small-point type with a laser printer (an inkjet will smear). Cut the accession numbers from the paper in narrow strips. Lay down a strip of B-72 (polyvinyl acetate) and lay the strip of paper with the accession number in the wet acrylic. When it dries lay down a protective layer on top.

Clothing and textiles should not be marked directly on the material. The best method is to sew a strip of cloth on the material and then write the number with a laundry pen. India ink will not work on textiles as it washes out, so use a laundry pen. Paper items should be marked with a soft pencil (#2). These are easily available in stationer's stores. You may not be able to mark coins, medallions, small jewelry items, small pieces of sculpture, etc., that do not have a surface on which it would be proper to place the marking. In the case of coins and medals you can buy special envelopes and mark the number on them. These envelopes are available in any coin shop. You can use small paper tags on jewelry. A small sculpture may have to be kept resting on a tag with its number. When the number is not placed on the object special care must be taken not to separate the tag from the object.

Glued-on paper labels, especially ones that are pressure sensitive, are a very poor choice. So are those neat long strips of plastic that you can number from a machine. The adhesives break down rapidly and may damage the object. The labels have a perverse way of dropping off at the most inconvenient moment, and then not being removable at other times. Clear cellophane or similar tapes should never be used.

Paper tags held on with string are very useful as a second marker but not as the permanent one. You can buy acid free ones from a number of sources such as library supply houses. Objects in storage will be easier to find with paper tags, and that may be a reason to use them. They should never be considered the sole means of marking objects as they are removed too easily.

Deaccessioning

The question in deaccessioning is not if there is going to be a problem, but when there will be one.[7]

With deaccessioning it is the *accessioning* policy that is important.

If you are careful what you bring in, you will have fewer objects of which to dispose. The development of a sound accession policy, the careful execution of procedures, and good records will put off the evil day, and lessen any problem with deaccessioning when it occurs. Moreover, there is hardly a museum in the country that does not depend on the goodwill of its audience for survival. That goodwill is often expressed in gifts to the museum. When offered objects the museum is under an obligation to accept only what it really needs, can really take care of, has a use for, and intends to keep.[8]

There is a "Justification for Accessions" form in appendix A (see A-3) that represents a procedure for evaluating objects *before* accessioning, and will help the museum make the decision to accept or reject items offered to it. It is a handy form to show collection committees. Using this procedure will help you acquire objects less likely to be deaccessioned later.

No matter how carefully written the collection policy of a museum may be, or how tightly that policy is enforced, there is no museum that does not occasionally end up with objects that do not belong in the collection:

- There may be too many of one kind of object.
- The object may not fit the collection policy.
- It may have deteriorated to the point where it has lost its integrity or is a threat to the collection.
- It may be a fake (or at least not as represented).
- The museum may not be able to take care of the object properly.

Balanced against these reasons for deaccessioning are some factors that may affect whether you can or cannot deaccession and how easy the process is:

- Provisions in your organic documents, such as your charter, constitution, or bylaws, may forbid or place restrictions on your ability to deaccession.
- Your agreement with the donor may disallow deaccessioning of that particular object, which normally could be deaccessioned.
- The donor, or his or her family, may still be alive and active in the community.
- The community may have an interest in the object(s) and create a public relations problem with the deaccession.

It is a poor policy for the museum to dispose of objects in its collection unless there is an overriding reason for doing so. I would recommend not deaccessioning an object from a living donor, or one that has a known history

---

Justification for Deaccession
   You have to document deaccessions very carefully and very thoroughly. This form can help all the parties involved visualize the reasons for deaccessioning an object. The form should contain these questions:
- Reason for deaccession,
  - Duplicates another object.
  - Not germane to the collection (does not fit the collection policy).
  - It is a fake, or not as represented.
  - It is in poor condition.
  - The museum cannot take care of it.
- Is the history of the object tied in any way to the purpose of the museum?
- Are there any restrictions on this object?
- Is the object part of a collection?
- Is the donor still living?
- Does the community have an interest in this object?
- What will happen to the object if it is not deaccessioned?
- What is the method of disposal?
- A place for all approvals of curator, director, collection committee, board, etc.
- Action taken.
- Date(s) of action.

Figure 9: Justification of Deaccession Form. This form captures all the reasons to deaccession or not to deaccession an object. Boards understand such a form. It is based on a form developed by Bruce Bazalon, former registrar of the Pennsylvania Historical and Museum Commission.

related to your purpose, unless it is deteriorated to the point it endangers the collection.

It is important to follow a set procedure in deaccessioning and to be able to justify all the steps. The Justification for Deaccessioning form (figure 9) makes sure you have considered all the factors when you deaccession an object. Each of the two collections policies in the appendix has a deaccession procedure including a Justification for Deaccessioning form. There should be a clearly understood policy about how the object is to be disposed of. Using the form, or the procedure it represents, will help the museum have a rational method of deaccessioning and keep the collection germane to the purpose of the museum.

When a museum sells a deaccessioned item, it is best to do this at public auction rather than private sale. This keeps things in the public eye. Private sales may give the perception of favoritism and self-dealing, serious ethical charges.

Deaccessioning Undocumented Objects
Undocumented objects are popularly called "found in the collection." You have the object but you do not know how you got it. Just because you do not

have any records of these objects does not mean you have the absolute right to dispose of them. Indeed, you may have to keep them almost forever. Some states have laws that set up a procedure for disposing of such objects. Advice from a lawyer is necessary.[9]

There is a rule in treating undocumented objects found in the collection: if they are not accessioned and you intend to dispose of them, then you do not need to accession them. It saves a lot of steps if you do not accession unknowns just to deaccession them. Disposal is much easier. It is mandatory, however, to make a list of these objects and get board approval when you dispose of them, so there is some record. You must also be very sure that these objects belong to you and are yours to dispose of. Several states have ways of acquiring title to such found-in-the-collection objects.

Documenting Deaccessions

When you take something into your collection, you should at the same time think about how it might be removed without creating confusion in the records. The governing body should make the deaccession policy a part of the registration manual. Any action to get rid of an object should be done only after the governing body acts. The easiest way to get such action is to have the curator, through the director, recommend to the collections committee that the object be deaccessioned. The committee then makes a report to the board concerning the object, the reasons for the deaccession, and the method of disposal. If the board approves, the action is carried out.

You should not get rid of the records for the object that has been deaccessioned just because it is gone. You are still obligated to keep the record of it. For paper records a note indicating that the object has been deaccessioned should be made in red ink in the master record. The reason for using red ink for this transaction on the records is that it will show up clearly. India ink should be used. The type of removal (sold, destroyed, transferred), the date it happened, and the date of the action of the governing body should all be entered into the permanent record. If you have catalogue cards for the deaccessioned object they should be placed in a dead file. There should be some method in a computer record to indicate that the object has been deaccessioned, and a method of keeping it from getting mixed with the rest of the records, but, again, the record should be kept. The status field (which tells whether it is an accession, loan, etc.) is good for this purpose.

Under both the AAM and AASLH ethics codes, funds received from the sale of accessioned items can go only to buy other artifacts (AAM and AASLH) or toward the conservation of objects in the collection (AASLH). This should be addressed in your collection policy.

Although the museum board should reserve the right to dispose of the collection in any way it sees fit, in actual practice the museum will be rated on how much it keeps and keeps well.

I could write a whole book on donor and community concerns involved in deaccessioning. The museum has to carefully consider what impact any deaccession will have on its relationship with its donors and the community. Every deaccession represents some failure on the part of the museum. However, deaccessioning is very much like pruning a tree; it hurts, but is necessary for growth. If the museum carefully considers each deaccession the problems will be fewer.

Tiered Collections

Museums often have objects that they wish to keep but do not wish to accession. Typical examples are objects that are used in education programs, or are kept for study. In these cases museums often create a tiered system. There may be anywhere from two to a dozen tiers. The museum designates one or two tiers in which the object is accessioned and cared for under the highest museum standards. Other tiers may not be technically accessioned, but may be used in education programs or kept as specimens. These often get a special numbering system or no numbering system at all and may be kept in different ledgers.

This arrangement will work, but the museum has to have a very good understanding of its mission and the role of the collection. The ability to administer such a system is important. Someone has to constantly monitor the use of objects so that everyone will understand that you can use objects marked with an "X" (for example) and may not use ones that are not.

Be aware that if you take in an object from a donor under the impression that it is to be a "museum" object and then place it in noncollection status you have created a sizable ethical and perhaps legal problem. Be up front with donors about the status of any object you take into your collection, whether accessioned or not.

What Not to Do and When Not to Do It

The major mistake people make is not to accession the object as soon as it comes in. If it is not accessioned promptly information will be lost, parts may turn up missing, or the object may not be accessioned at all. I have always been amazed, at the museums where I had collection responsibilities, how many objects sat around for years without being accessioned. The final mistake is not to put the number on the object at the same time it is accessioned.

The Final Word on Accessioning

Several variations of the basic system of accessioning have been outlined here in the hope that an understanding of them will help the person in charge set up his or her own system. The important things about any system are

- That the flow of actions be orderly and uncomplicated from the first contact until the object is displayed or stored
- That the museum be able to account for any action at any stage of the process
- That the system be consistent
- That the system have the understanding and approval of the people directing and managing the museum and be able to be carried out over a number of years through the reigns of several curators

The records of the museum are only tools meant to help you preserve and interpret the collection. Do not create a monster that will eat up the purpose of the museum in a maze of paperwork. Simplicity is the key.

Notes

1. Stephen L. Williams, "Critical Concepts Concerning Non-Living Collections," *Collections* 1 (2004), 37–66, in particular "Accessioning," 43–45 and "Cataloging," 45–46.

2. Malaro, *Primer*, 52–137.

3. You can also get a type of record called a "minute book," which has loose pages. The pages can be permanently fixed later, but can be written upon or copied until bound.

4. For the reasons for not making the accession record a card, see chapter 6 on catalogues.

5. James C. Blackaby, Chair, Common Data Bases Task Force, *Final Report to the Field, September 1989*, Common Agenda for History Museums (Nashville: American Association for State and Local History, 1989).

6. The marking of objects is a constantly evolving technology. Terry Segal, "Collections Management: Marking," in Buck and Gilmore, *New Museum Registration Methods*, 65–94; Helen Alten, "Materials for Labeling Collections," *The Upper Midwest Museums Collections Care Network* 1, no. 6 (Winter 1996), 1–7. The Registrars Committee of AAM keeps abreast of developments. You can join by contacting them at AAM.

7. The quote about accessions being a potential problem was once a commonplace in the museum field. I have not heard it lately, but it is true.

8. Stephen E. Weil, *A Deaccession Reader* (Washington, DC: American Association of Museums, 1997), *passim*; Phelan, *Museum Law*, 302–306; Charles Philips, "The Ins and Outs of Deaccessioning," *History News* 38 (November 1983), 6–11; Malaro, *Primer*, 138–155; Martha Morris, "Deaccessions," in Buck and Gilmore, *New Museum Registration Methods*, 167–176; The New York Association of Museums, "Guidelines on Deaccessioning," is shown in Phelan, pp. 241–242.

9. Buck and Gilmore, "Found in the Collection," *Collection Conundrums*, 37–47. They have a state-by-state chart of laws effecting found-in-the-collection objects.

CHAPTER FIVE

~

Documentation

When you acquire an object you acquire a great deal more than the object itself. You acquire the history of the people who made or used the object. This legacy is often more valuable to the museum than the intrinsic value of the object. The very difference between a history museum and other types of museums is often that they collect objects for their historical value rather than their intrinsic, aesthetic, or scientific values. Of course these other values are important, and a major factor in history museum collections, but not the primary value. The only way to preserve this value is to write it down. This written history is the documentation of the object and the collection.

In the United States it is a normal practice to separate registration from documentation. The usual practice is to consider that registration applies to all the records generated in the acquisition, accession, and catalogue process and that documentation applies to research developed on the object and the collection. Be aware that some people in the museum field apply the term "documentation" to all the documents developed on an accession or the collection. They expressly include the ones I separate as "registration" documents. This usage is more true of Great Britain than the United States, although the term "documentation" as applied to registration is often used here. I am separating the two terms in this book, partly to follow the common practice in the United States, and partly to avoid confusion. For the purposes of this book "documentation" is part of the registration process, not the process itself.[1]

You acquire information on the object in two ways. Some information comes with the object. The rest is found by research.

Information That Comes with the Object

The donor or seller of an object will often furnish you with information about the object. There will often be the owner's reminiscences or family history. If you question the donor he or she can often give you an amazing amount of background information. It is important to capture all of this history that you can. Ask for photographs, documents, and other things related to the object. The owner will not know they are important.

You should be aware of all the pitfalls of oral information. Nothing ever became less important or less valuable over time. Still, if it is the original owner or a descendent who provides the information, it is close to the source. Almost all oral information is lost when the object is sold to a dealer or second party. Any history coming from such second-party sources is suspect, especially if it is an unsupported attribution to an owner, artist, or maker.

However unlikely some of this information may be, if you do not collect it at the time of the accession it will be forever lost. All of it should be carefully recorded. You can check out the information later through research.

Information Discovered by Research

The museum should have an ongoing research project concerning the history covered by the museum's purpose. If your purpose is to preserve the history of Hero County you would continually conduct research on the history of the county. Research is never completed.

You also must conduct research on the objects in the museum. Who made or used them, when they made them, and how they were used will be constant objects of research. You must also learn something about the cultural and aesthetic motives of the people who made and used the objects, and the technical qualities of the object. Research will give you a greater understanding of the people associated with your collection, and be of enormous help in collecting more objects, interpretation, and exhibits.

Registration Files versus Research Files

Even the smallest museum may have several types of documents that ought to be preserved. It is common to have the accession file that contains all the documents on each object, a research file that contains research on the history related to the museum's purpose, the archives that contain documents in the museum's collection, and the museum files that are business and other records.[2] There is a good reason to keep separate files but all of these should be preserved as museum archives.

The major difference between archives and business files is the type of care they receive and how you intend to preserve them. The archives, of whatever kind, are part of the museum's collection. Although archives are used for research, they receive the highest standard of care the museum can devise. It may be stored separately, but the museum registration system is part of the museum's archives. Sometimes research files are files that do not receive the same care that the archives do. In this case, you should make sure that documents that are to be preserved go into the archives or at least get a high standard of care.

Documents that come with objects are part of the museum archives. If these are stored in accession files be sure that these files follow archive standards. If the documents are used frequently, then they should be copied, the copies placed in the research files, and the originals preserved.

Some documents are as much a part of the accession as the object itself. These might be operating manuals, original letters referring to the object, photographs that show the object in use, legal documents concerning it, etc. You have to make a decision on which of these are accessioned, which go into the accession file, which go into the research file, and which go to the museum archives. The decision is based on the standard of care you give each file and, perhaps, who has access to it.

The Museum Library

The museum should develop a library on its collection. A small book budget will go a long way. If you collect a book here and there, eventually you will have a good reference library. Books are expensive, but many are remaindered and can be acquired cheaply. Donors are often quite generous with books. When I started at Old Economy I had eight books in the museum reference library. When I left sixteen years later there were over two thousand books in the library, and I never, in that whole time, had a book budget. If I had a book budget I would have had four thousand books. Keep at it, and eventually your efforts will show results.

Publishing Research

No research is any good unless it is published. The museum publishes in many ways. Exhibits and interpretation programs can be considered a method of publication that is especially suited to a museum. Every exhibit requires some research and if this is published it will add another dimension to the exhibit. As simple a thing as a fact sheet will outlast the exhibit and be a permanent remainder of your research. Even if these have to be done on the office copier, they are still a publication. The museum should publish articles and monographs on its collection. Your newsletter is a good place to publish what you have found. Another way to publish is to encourage and assist outside researchers. Their publications should be added to your library.

Remember that exhibits and interpretation programs, although valuable and necessary, are ephemeral, but publications last forever.

Interest Groups

There is an interest group on almost any subject, no matter how obscure. I once subscribed to a magazine for plumb bob collectors. These groups have publications, meetings, memberships, etc. There must be at least one, if not a dozen, of these groups whose interests are aligned with those of any museum. These groups will be conversant with current research and standards in their field. They will know all the specialists in the obscure areas of their interest. They will know all the good books on their specialty and how to get discounts.

I would suggest that you join as many of these interest groups as you need and can afford. Go to as many of their meetings as you can. Their annual meetings are information factories where you can find out almost anything you need to know. You will discover the state of current knowledge when you do this.

Information from Other Museums

Other museums that collect in the same area as yours can be quite helpful. They will have a research file and a library. Their professional staff will be conversant with the knowledge you need. Museums lend objects as well, and may be able to help you with exhibits.

On the other hand, it is a common experience in a large museum for someone from the Godforsaken Historical Society to show up unannounced at the most inconvenient moment and seek highly specialized knowledge. The seeker might be put off by curt answers and hasty references to standard reference works, but you can hardly expect curators to impart all the knowledge they have gained in a lifetime in twenty minutes. Contact the museum in advance, tell the staff what you would like to know, and you will usually find them very helpful.

The Internet offers museums access to a huge pool of information about objects and collections. However, its very size offers a challenge.

Higher Standards

The history museum profession is now placing a much higher value on capturing the historical data on the object than it has in the past. The very nature of a history museum, of being more interested in the object's history than in the object as a specimen, makes this an imperative.

What Not to Do and When Not to Do It

The first mistake is not to get all the information at the time you acquire the object. The second mistake is not to write it down. I once ran a museum with almost eighty thousand objects related to a particular culture. Each object had a story, but that story was lost as it was in the heads of the founders, who had died thirty years before. It is a general rule that if you do not capture the information at first, it is lost forever. Since the history museum may be more interested in the history of the object than the object itself, you have an obligation to find out all you can about the object and write this down in some easily accessible form. If you have done this on every object, you may have preserved something as valuable as the object itself.

Note

1. The common view in the United States is that documentation is the assemblage of all the research information on the object. Europeans view it as all the documents assembled during the whole registration process. I tend to accept the former view. See Museum Documentation Association, *Practical Museum Documentation*, 2nd ed. (Duxford, Cambridgeshire, UK: Museum Documentation Association, 1981). However, one of the first practical books aimed at American museums, Carl E. Guthe, *The Management of Small History Museums*, 2nd ed. (Nashville: AASLH, 1969), 21–50, discusses the entire registration system as documentation.

2. William A. Deiss, *Museum Archives: An Introduction* (Chicago: Society of American Archivists, 1984), discusses museum archives as separate from other archives; James Sumerville, "Using, Managing and Preserving the Records of Your Historical Organization," *Technical Report 11* (Nashville: AASLH, 1986).

CHAPTER SIX

~

The Catalogue

Cataloguing: Creation of a full record on information about a specimen or artifact, cross-referenced to other records and files, including the process of identifying and documenting these objects in detail.[1]

The catalogue[2] is the mechanism that allows you to extract useful information from the museum records. The catalogue divides the information in your records into useful classes or categories and provides the tool for access to this data. At one time this mechanism would have been a card file. With the advent of the computer the concept of what a museum catalogue is has been expanded and access to both the records and the collection has been greatly extended. Despite this, the card catalogue survives in many museums—some are even generated by a computer. Regardless of the radically different media used in storing catalogues there is not a lot of difference among them in the type of data stored. It is difficult to discuss paper and electronic methods separately so I am going to discuss them together.

The term "catalogue" comes from the ancient Greek and means to count down, with the idea of counting completely. The first catalogues, as we know them, were developed in the Hellenistic period in the famous library at Alexandria. One of the interesting concepts was developed by a man named Callimachus who arrange the catalogue by author in alphabetical order—a revolutionary idea at the time. Libraries have been thinking about catalogues ever since. The first museum ledgers that we know about were developed in the renaissance. These listed the objects in some arbitrary order, usually the order received, in a journal. Early attempts at cataloguing included keeping separate ledgers for different types of objects or for different collections.[3]

A paper catalogue takes some thought to develop and a lot of work to maintain. Using the search and sort functions of a computer one can easily generate an endless number of types of catalogues.

Until relatively recently, a ledger was the preferred method of storing paper collection records. An accession ledger (whether written or electronic), accession sheets, and similar forms store almost all the information the museum has on its collection in their mass. They are useful records, and one would hardly have been considered a museum without them, but it is very difficult to easily extract data from them. The catalogue is the easy and safe access to all this information.

It would be interesting to know who the genius was that first took the information in the accession ledger, wrote out each record on a separate piece of paper or card, and arranged these into categories to give useful information. If we knew who that person was, we should erect a statue of him or her, because he or she solved the problem of how to access the huge mass of information in the museum's records. The cards could be placed in endless combinations allowing for almost limitless searches for the information in the museum records. It was as revolutionary an idea as Callimachus arranging the catalogue alphabetically by author in the third century BC.

The cards were also a curse. They multiplied like flies, they were difficult to create, the files occupied a lot of space, the cards stored endless amounts of redundant data, there were multiple forms, people mixed them up, lost them, and misplaced them, and inaccurate data was safely ensconced in their depths.

Computers and Cataloguing

A computer can create any kind of catalogue the mind can imagine and it is faster and easier than any paper catalogue. I would not recommend creating a paper catalogue anymore. The only reasons for discussing paper catalogues at all is to discuss the type of reports (catalogues) you need, some museums still have older paper catalogues, and a few museums still create paper catalogues from the digital records.[4]

The computer's ability to search for, sort, and index data, its ability to pull together related pieces of information, the lack of redundancy, and especially the speed make the computer the ultimate cataloguing tool. One big advantage of the computer is that you need few, if any, forms. Instead of having information stored on a number of pieces of paper and these in a number of places, the computer can store the information in one place to which access is a lot faster and easier. Inaccurate information is even more of a problem in a computer than in a card file, but the computer can often identify some of its own errors.

I do not use a card catalogue anymore. I can extract more useful information from my data bank, either on the screen or by a written report, than could easily be extracted from any card catalogue.

Even with a computer, however, a card catalogue may have uses. A card might be considered an analog while a computer is digital. When there is a problem, you can spread all the doubtful cards on the desk and see the whole problem. With a computer, you usually can see only one record at a time. When the computer is down, the card catalogue is a good backup. When you need just one or two objects from storage, it is much easier to take a card or two with you rather than a thick printout. If the collection is static and does not change much, a card catalogue might be useful. If there is limited access to the computer, a card catalogue might be a supplement to the computer, allowing more people admission to the records. If the collection is small, a card catalogue might be a lot easier to use than a computer. A card catalogue can provide safe public access to the records. Finally, some people are more comfortable with paper records than electronic ones.

On the other hand, if the collection is large, is constantly growing, or is audited frequently, or the records are being updated, or one needs to make sophisticated searches, a computer data bank will be a lot more useful than a paper catalogue. If you have a large collection, you may wish to consider if you want to have a paper catalogue at all.

I expect to see the catalogue card almost completely replaced by the computer in my lifetime, if that has not happened already.

Cataloguing Involves Two Different Concepts

Considering the time people spend cataloguing a museum collection, the definition of the act of cataloguing is rather vague and there is no agreement on the meaning. There are actually several different processes that are called cataloguing. They mainly fall into two classes:

1. The creation of the catalogue by extracting data from your records and presenting it in some useful format.
2. The updating of the information in the collection records. Every generation of professionals that works with the collection expands the museum's knowledge about the collection. If this new understanding of

the collection is written into the permanent records it will destroy primary data. Therefore, the new information is written into the catalogue. Often a completely new catalogue is created and then becomes the record of choice. When people talk about cataloguing they are usually talking about this updating process.

When you enter new data into a catalogue you may be destroying some of the old information. This old information may be valuable. To get around this problem the museum should archive the old paper records or periodically archive a copy of its computer records. For most museums, archiving the computer records once every year is enough. For large active collections that are constantly being updated more often may be necessary, say every month or even once a day.

What Does the Catalogue Tell You?

What does a catalogue tell you? That depends on what you need to know. Some questions can be fairly obscure, such as "What objects are there, and where are they located, which tell me something about the Industrial Revolution in Hero County?" Some questions are fairly simple, such as "Where are all the Windsor chairs?" Others are more complicated, such as "Is there a relationship between tapered legs and lipped drawers on tables made in Hero County before 1810?" Even a paper catalogue can give you this information, though it may be harder to dig out than it would be from a computer.

Classification

No catalogue system will work well unless there is at least one constant used to classify the objects. The reason for this is that the constant gives you the ability to classify the whole file in some rational order. Using a constant you can deal with the collection as a whole. Different disciplines use different classification criteria:

- Art museums use artist, but also period, medium, or genre.
- Natural history museums use a taxonomy based a system first developed by Linnaeus (Karl Linné, 1707–1778).
- Earth science museums use geological epochs or chemical composition.
- History museums, until recently, did not have a classification system.

The favored classifications in history museums for many years was such things as the material of which the object was made (such as "silver"), or broad topical classes ("tools"), or style ("Hepplewhite"), or, in large museums, the departments that were responsible for the collections ("Social History").

It was not until Robert Chenhall created his system in the 1970s that the idea of a systematic catalogue in a history museum came about.[5] The system would be a standard taxonomy common across the whole history field and useful to anyone. To a great extent, Chenhall's dream of a systematic classification system has been widely adopted by the history museum field. I will refer to the *Revised Edition* (Blackaby) as *Nomenclature*. This system of classification arranges objects by their use and has simple naming conventions. By using *Nomenclature* you can arrange your collection in a meaningful order that is understandable by any rational person.

The reason for using a widely accepted classification system is that it is readily understandable by many people in the museum field. A new curator, or a visiting scholar, will be able to understand your system with little instruction. Besides, *Nomenclature* is fairly simple. If the museum develops its own classification system, it may be a lot harder to learn, and may not be consistent over many changes of staff.

There are new systems that challenge the concept that you need a constant for a registration system. The cry is to let the computer make its own classification. If there is the right kind of data, many systems can do just that. Please note that numbering systems are not a classification system even though you can arrange your system by number. It is just a method of registering each object.

How *Nomenclature* Works

Nomenclature classifies a collection based on how the objects are used. It has the terms arranged in a taxonomy.[6]

If you know a bit about furniture, you might describe a typical large case piece as either a Kass, a Schrank, a wardrobe, a press, an armoire, or whatever. Even if the catalogue entries bearing these terms were all filed under "wardrobe" this is bound to cause confusion. A person from the part of the country I come from will call a certain iron cooking utensil a "skillet," while someone from a less-fortunate part might call it a "frying pan." Both terms are correct. Do you drive a car or an automobile? The number of synonyms does not matter in speaking or writing, but does when you are classifying your collection. *Nomenclature* uses only one term for each object. Furthermore, these terms are arranged in broad families based on their use. This allows you to find records quickly. Unlike many of the old classification systems, certain types of objects could appear in every one of *Nomenclature's* families. Most trades or skills use a hammer. These hammers are each filed separately under their use, while in the old days they would all be filed together under "hammers."

Nomenclature systematizes the naming of terms we use in identifying man-made objects. The system is not particularly difficult to adopt, even for a small museum. You have to recognize that Chenhall did not create just a list of approved terms, but a whole system of classification of objects for history museums.

As an example you may have five common bench planes: a smoothing plane, a jack plane, a fore plane, a jointer, and a long jointer. Filed alphabetically by these names they would be scattered in several places in the catalogue:

fore plane (in the *F*s)
jack plane (in the *J*s)
jointer plane (in the *J*s)
long jointer (in the *L*s)
smoothing plane (in the *S*s)

This would make searches difficult, at best, as you would have to know exactly what you were looking for in order to find it. However, if you followed the principles in *Nomenclature* and treated the noun as a genus (class) and the modifier as a species (type), you would have them arranged thusly:

plane, fore
plane, jack
plane, jointer
plane, long jointer
plane, smoothing

If you use Chenhall's families these tools would be filed under a family name of "Tools and Equipment for Materials, Woodworking," so you would always be able to find them in one particular place, so long as you knew their use.

It is true that the nature of the English language causes a few problems. Such objects as a teaspoon ("spoon, tea"?) or a football ("ball, foot"?) will not neatly arrange themselves. There are alternate spellings which create a consistency problem. In the worst cases you can use a cross-reference.

Object Number	Object Names	Object Summary
09266	Assembly, Latch	Door Latch
13297	Assembly, Latch	Board with Wooden Latch
18284	Assembly, Latch	Heavy Knob Latch
19430	Assembly, Latch	Blake Latch Assembly
15060	Assembly, Latch	Wishbone Spring Latch Assembly
15480	Assembly, Latch	Keyhole Latch Assembly
03511	Assembly, Latch	Partial Assembly Latch: Bar
08359	Assembly, Latch	Norfolk Latch Assembly
08529	Assembly, Latch	Bar Latch Assembly
05980	Assembly, Latch	Square Plate Latch Assembly
05983	Assembly, Latch	Suffolk Latch Assembly
05083	Assembly, Latch	Keyhole Latch Assembly
05086	Assembly, Latch	Spring Latch Assembly
07161	Assembly, Latch	Dutch Door Catch
F.80.186.01	Hat	Boater Hat
F.80.187.01	Hat	Straw Boater
F.80.192.01	Hat	Cloth Hat
15778	Hat, Fireman's	Kensington Fire Company Parade Hat
15766	Hat, Fireman's	Northern Liberty Fire Company No. 1 Parade Hat
15770	Hat, Fireman's	Friendship Fire Company Parade Hat
04781	Hat, Fireman's	Monroe Fire Company No. 33 Parade Hat
11470	Lock, Door	American-type Door Lock
04009	Lock, Door	Spring Door Lock
03040	Lock, Door	Carpenter-type Rim Door Lock
25001	Lock, Door	Plate Stock Lock
03039	Lock, Door	German Door Lock
15077	Lock, Door	Mortise Door Lock
09165	Lock, Door	Plate-type Door Lock
15069	Lock, Door	Moravian Door Lock
13993	Lock, Door	Bambury-type Door Lock
13855	Lock, Door	Cabinet Rim Lock
02353	Lock, Door	Door Lock
03390	Lock, Door	Door Lock and Key
06653	Lock, Door	German-type Door Lock and Key
25731	Sampler	Alphabet Sampler
12027	Sampler	Buckingham School Alphabet Sampler
01797	Sampler	Motif Sampler
85.15.001	Sampler	Union Academy Doylestown Alphabet and Verse Sampler
16564	Sampler	Westtown School Verse Sampler
01537	Sampler	Verse Sampler

Figure 10: Computer-Generated Lexicon. With a computer there is no reason to generate a complete list of terms for the whole collection, but just what is needed as in the example. Courtesy of the Mercer Museum, Bucks County Historical Society.

Unless you have an unusually complex system I do not think you need a lexicon, that is, a dictionary, a list of terms. If you do need a lexicon then setting one up is simple. If you have a computer, you can generate a word list that will be the basis of a lexicon. Some systems will do word counts for you that will simplify the process. It is a little more difficult with a manual system. A relatively easy way for a museum to set up a lexicon with a manual system is to go through your catalogue. Each term should be compared against *Nomenclature's* list. If it is not on the list then you have to create a term. *Nomenclature* explains how to do this. Enter the term on a card. This will help with later descriptions. You need to enter each term only once. In a collection of fifteen thousand items I used only about five hundred terms while *Nomenclature* lists over five thousand. (See figure 10.)

Some museums have a separate listing of their catalogue headings. These listings often become part of the registrar's manual or the operating procedures of the museum. That helps avoid duplication, is especially handy with large staff, and may be necessary if the museum is developing a nomenclature. However, I really do not think a small museum has to worry about listing its headings separately. That is just one more thing to take care of, and if you really want to know what your headings are, you can look in the catalogue drawer, or in your computer's data bank. *Nomenclature* supplies a set of ready-made headings for you.

If you color-code your dividing cards, so that you can tell the main heading from the subheadings, it is easier. Cards are filed by accession number inside each classification.

Alternates to *Nomenclature*

There is an alternate to *Nomenclature*. There are such things as "authority lists" or "vocabularies."[7] These are lists of approved terms. *The Art and Architecture Thesaurus* is best known of this type in the museum field. Most have several approved terms for every type of object. Indeed several have every possible term. Most authority lists are for specific types of collections. They are too large and cumbersome for small museums, approaching the size of unabridged dictionaries in some cases. Unless you have an exceedingly unusual collection I would not recommend them for small museums.

What Catalogues Do You Need?

If you follow the concepts in this book, the basic records of your museum registration system that we have developed so far will consist of

- Transfer of title document consisting of a gift agreement, bill of sale, or some other document transferring title to the museum.
- Accessions register containing the accession number, brief description of what is in the accession, the source, the method of acquisition, and the date of acquisition. The ledger may serve as this document.
- Accession record on each object in the accession. This would include all the information you have on the object. Paper accession records should be bound into an accession ledger or book.
- Accession file consisting of correspondence, research notes, documents, and other records of each accession in a file.

You will need all these records if you are writing them into a bound ledger with a quill pen, or typing them into a paperless system on a computer, or every technique in between. I am convinced that I could get a small museum accredited by the American Association of Museums with no more collection records than these primary records, provided the records were complete and accurate. However, as I have emphasized several times, you do not wish to continually use your primary records. The catalogue is the device that not only protects these records but gives you access to them.

I am going to discuss manual (or paper) catalogues separately from ones generated by computer.

Manual Catalogues
It is impossible to advise anyone on which catalogues to have without talking to him or her and seeing the museum and its needs. I suggest the following catalogues are the minimum that any museum needs.

Main Entry Catalogue
A main entry is the card or record upon which any other type of record in the catalogue is modeled. In fact, the easiest way to make other catalogues is to copy the main entry card. (See figure 11.)

The main entry card contains most of the catalogue information. Just what the catalogue information is, is mostly up to you, but it would logically consist of the accession number, the source, and the descriptive information. This type of information is discussed in chapter 4. If you have only one catalogue, use a main entry card, and all of your cards arranged by *Nomenclature's* principles, then you can answer such complicated questions as "What furniture do we have that was made in Hero County before 1800 by known cabinetmakers?" When you can answer that kind of sophisticated question from the main entry catalogue, you have to question the wisdom of having several.[8]

Object: Plate, Dinner   **Acc. No.**: 52.2.1
Class.: 04 Food Service
Source: Ivy Propan
Location: 101
Material: Pottery   **Size**: 11.375 dia. x .875
Maker: Clews   **Place**: England
Date: ca. 1830   **Association**: Lafayette

Description:
Flat Bowl with curving sides; marly curves up; lip faintly
scalloped; foot ring; underglaze blue transfer of landing of
Lafayette over white ground; on bottom is stamp between two
circles, "Clews Warranted safe [illegible]"; and, in underglaze
blue, "The Landing of Lafayette at Castle Garden New York 16th
August 1824".

HERO COUNTY HISTORICAL MUSEUM

Figure 11: **Main Entry Card. This card contains only the information for most searches.
The name of the museum is at the bottom so more useful information can be accessed
from the top.**

If there are photographs of the collection, the place to put one of them is
on the main entry card. It saves looking in another catalogue for an image.

The Source or Donor Catalogue
The second of the catalogues necessary to operate the museum is the donor
or source catalogue. Keep in mind that the sources of funds for purchases are
also donors. You may wish to keep a list of vendors as well. Museums that depend on donors for most of their accessions will find themselves constantly
using such a file. It is easy to make up, since all you need is a brief description of the accession and the accession number. All the other information is
in the accession records. A donor card might look like those shown in figures
12, 13, and 14.

The example in figure 14 is from a three-number system. On the single-
number (figure 12) and two-number systems (figure 13), you would have to
enter a range of numbers that cover the accession.

The donor cards can easily be made up periodically, such as at the end of
the month. There should only be one card for each source.

Sarah Bellum

28-132
345-362
421-447
1002

Figure 12:   Single-Number Donor Card

Minerva Apolis

56.3-.9
62.32-.33
75.12-.14
1002

Figure 13:   Two-Number Donor Card

Truck, Mr. & Mrs. Mack (Dorothy)

56.36   Toolbox and tools
62.33   Garments, family papers, photos
75.8   Dining room table and chairs
82.27   Misc. household items 1925-1940
93.21   Mrs. Truck's wedding dress

Figure 14:   Three-Number Donor Card

Tracking Location

Because good museum practice requires that you place your hands on any object at short notice, one of the things you need to know is the location of each object in your museum. The standard method is to write the location in pencil on your main entry card. Every time you move the object you change the location. This can be a complicated and time-consuming task.

Another method is to have a card on each object filed by location. When you move the object you move the card. This is handy when someone asks you about the spittoon in the main room or when doing inventories; you can find the card you need quite easily. The problem with a separate card file for location is that you cannot find the location from the main entry catalogue, so you still have to have the location in pencil on that card, as well, which means you are keeping the location in two places. If you can support that, a separate location catalogue is quite handy. One of the advantages of a computerized registration system is its ability to easily generate a location catalogue.

Partly to resolve these problems, and partly because you can not write a location on a computer record in pencil, a system of having objects "live" at one location was developed. The object is assigned a permanent location where it "lives." The only time the location is tracked is when the object is moved. This system has a lot to recommend it.

Whether you have a separate location catalogue or not, it is useful to have a catalogue of each exhibit room. These are handy references when visitors ask questions. There are several ways to do this. One is to keep a card file in the room containing a copy of the main entry card. If the object is moved so is the card. Most museums using this system favor small ring-bound books as they are easy to hide, yet handy. A computer can generate a report with the objects arranged by location, on short notice.

An exhibit catalogue is a permanent record of what was in the exhibit. It can be in any form, but it may be best typed up on sheets and filed with the other material on the exhibit. The simplest is to xerox the cards onto a sheet of paper. I generate a complete catalogue of the items in each exhibit from my data bank. If a question comes up, I can then find all the information I need in one place. In the old days I xeroxed the catalogue cards of objects on exhibit.

I discuss a method of marking individual electronic records with a flag so you can pull a group of them, perhaps for an exhibit, in the chapter on computers.

Association Catalogue

Part of the information that gives an object value is its association with people, places, or events. The association is often more important than the ob-

```
Gomorra Pool Hall
Main Street, Hero (1929-1979)

62.29.27        Pool Cue
70.2.3          Snooker championship cup
77.38.1         photo of "gang" at hall
76.99.8         Scrapbook of trial

Cross Ref. Lott, G.D. (owner), Main Street, Recreation, Billiard Halls

              HERO COUNTY HISTORICAL SOCIETY
```

Figure 15: Association Card

ject. A silk hat is a silk hat, but if had been Abraham Lincoln's silk hat . . . !
An object may have a manufacturer's name on it or may be associated with
a particular event, such as the Civil War, or with a particular place, such as
the local reform school. An easy way to access the knowledge of this association can be a valuable aid in research and developing exhibits. An association catalogue can help you do this. (See figure 15.)

Association cards are somewhat like donor cards, but they have to have
the title of the object as well as the name of the association and the accession numbers. A typical example would look like the figure above.

When you plan to make an exhibit on Main Street or on recreation in
Hero, or on pool halls, or on G. D. Lott, you can look up the information in
your association file. This file is easier to make up if you note the association
on your accession record. Even if you cannot make up an association file now,
the information will be readily available when you can.

Images of the Collection

Photographs and Digital Images

The trite old saying about a picture being worth a thousand words is particularly true of a registration system. An image of the object makes any description much clearer and can help greatly in identifying objects. Images are
also useful in showing condition.[9] I would not recommend using film as digital images have pretty much replaced it.

Equipment to take good images of the collection is readily available, in-
expensive, and easy to operate. If the museum staff does not have the expertise or time, there are many people who do who can be asked to take images as a volunteer activity. It is best to take an image of each object in the

collection as it is accessioned. If that is impossible, try to take an image of the more important objects.

The purpose of the photograph is for identification. Although a good photograph is desirable, you are not turning out a work of art. The picture's main purpose is identification. Each object should be photographed individually, as it is almost impossible to photograph a group of objects well enough for identification purposes. If you are still using film, a contact print should be made of the negative from each frame and the negative fastened in a sleeve on the back. These sleeves are readily available from archive supply houses.

If you have a film archive of your collection one way to have a catalogue is to have a print made of each object the same size as the file drawer, say three by five inches, and file them in accession number order. The information you need can be printed on the back. If you have a rubber stamp made containing the information you need, the job becomes much easier. With a computer you can generate a label that will do the same thing. The negative is more important than the prints, so keeping track of them is important. You should never use a rubber stamp on historic photographs and documents. You will find that a digital image is a much easier way, and cheaper than film.

There are a number of ways to store images electronically. These systems are very valuable as you can bring up the image with the catalogue record. The technology is evolving rapidly and is getting cheaper and easier to use. These electronically stored images can be called up along with the catalogue records, and give your audience access to the collection without having to handle the objects.[10]

The size of the record is a factor in digital images. Black and white images take up a lot less memory than color, but color gives a dimension to the image not found in black and white. Keep the color images to about sixteen colors in a JPEG or similar format and they will take up less room.

Remember that electronically stored data does not have an infinite shelf life—in fact, it is relatively short—while a properly made and stored photograph on archive-quality paper has a long life. It may be very difficult to convert an image from one format to another, although a majority of programs will read most of the imaging conventions. However, CD disks, if they are not on the way to obsolescence, may be more permanent than even a photograph on good paper, *so long as there is hardware and software to read them.*

They now have digital "movie" cameras (camcorders) that are relatively cheap and easy to use. The make a good image of the collection and one can make comments on certain aspects of the collection as one goes along. Keep in mind that any electronic image will deteriorate with time. One can make good copies of photos or digital images on archive-quality paper. The old VCR will work but its technology is on the way out.

The Physical Catalogue

You can get cards from library supply houses. I favor a larger card, such as four by six inches, which holds a great deal more information than the standard three-by-five-inch card. However, they are harder to find in the right card stock and it is difficult to get file cabinets for them. The ubiquitous three-by-five-inch card is readily available and the file cabinets for them are obtainable from many sources. Since card file cabinets get a great deal of use they should be of good quality.

In the days when every card had to be typed by hand, typing them on good card stock made sense because you expected the card to last forever. Now that even the smallest museum will have access to a word processor, a cheaper stock might be used. As records are updated the old cards are thrown out and new ones generated. Some museums generate a whole new card catalogue periodically, and archive the old one.

Each object should have its own card, except in cases of pairs or small sets of less than, say, five items.

Even a small museum will need a large number of cards. Printing a form on them can be expensive. For this reason I am recommending that only one type of card be printed, although it is possible to place all the information on a blank card. This is the main entry card. You can use the same card form for several different types of catalogues.

Typing catalogue cards is a real chore. Any step you can take to reduce the work is worth the effort. It is a good idea to arrange the data on the worksheet (see appendix A-4) in the same order that it is typed on the cards. This will promote accuracy as well as speed up the process. You can also buy almost any size card in a continuous strip that will fit most typewriters or printers. Most data managers are able to print forms and cards or to send data to a form created with a word processor. This can be configured in any form you find useful. Some people do not use a computer but type catalogue cards into a word processor. I raise the question that if you can type all those records into a word processor, why can't you type them into a data management program? The cost for either program is about the same.

Catalogues without Cards

There are catalogues without cards. One kind is a computer catalogue. Some museums have very static collections or static exhibits. In such instances, it is often easier to list the information on sheets of paper. These "page catalogues" are kept in file drawers or loose-leaf binders and can easily be copied on any office copier. The big disadvantage is that a change in any item affects the whole catalogue.

I have discussed paper catalogues chiefly in terms of cards. The advantage of cards over lists on paper is that cards can be easily shuffled and a change on one card does not affect the whole list.

Computer Catalogues

You need the same kind of information from a computer catalogue that you need from a card file; it is just stored differently. There should be some assurance that your program can extract the information you want and present it in some usable form on both screen and paper. These reports are substitutes for the old paper catalogues. Most data management programs can be made to configure almost any kind of report using the data in its data bank.

You need to be able to access the information you need. You might wish to generate a list of all the silver in storage, which would make searches a lot easier. You might have the list sorted by accession number, location, donor, and title. These will do very well as catalogues. You have an advantage in that you can often take a printout of the whole catalogue (or the computer itself) with you when you go out into collection storage. The corrected data can be entered into your computer every so often and keep the master record complete and accurate. However, if you want them, the computer can just as easily be made to generate cards.

Again, size of the collection plays a part in whether you generate paper catalogues from the computer. It is much easier for a small collection to have a printout than a large museum. Generating 3,000 cards with the typical office printer may be more than a day's work; generating 100,000 pages may take better than a month. Even simple reports, where each record takes up only one line, can be quite extensive. A complete report of one line of data for each record for a collection of 10,000 objects might well take up over 200 pages. Still, that is less than the seven or so drawers a card catalogue of the same size collection might take. Most museums with a data bank, if they generate paper records at all, use them for specific tasks, such as inventory, and use the computer for cataloguing.

Using the Description as a Catalogue Device

A computer gives you a big advantage in its ability to search out information anywhere in the record. If you use the same standards of *Nomenclature* in the material you put in the description field, rather than in a number of fields, you can cut the amount of work necessary to enter and maintain data and can extract a lot more information. From this you can easily pick out such things as all the gouges with inside bevels, or what percentage has sockets rather than tangs. If you have a similar worksheet for furniture, you can easily pick up all the case pieces with lipped drawers. I was once asked for all the tables with an outside taper on the legs, an easy question to answer if the information is there.

I discuss computers in chapter 8. For now, you should make sure that the program can edit, sort, index, or otherwise compile the information you need from your record and present it in some usable form.

Inventories

The inventory is used to check the accuracy of the information you have on each object, its condition, and its location.[11] Catalogues will stay up to date only if there is a periodic inventory. The ideal is to inventory your collection once a year. This may be beyond the capabilities of a small museum, but if you do about a third of the museum each year you will have examined the whole collection every three years. I would bet the mortgage that any collection that has not been inventoried in the last three years has numerous problems with its registration system.

There is the problem of the large collection. A collection of 10,000 objects may take two teams several days to inventory, but what about a collection of 100,000 objects? In this situation, it may be necessary to take a "spot" inventory. This inventory only looks a small portion of the collection so see if there are problems. You might take 1000 records at random and see if you can find the objects and see if their records are up to date. Then pick 1000 objects from several areas and examine their records. If there are few problems this will give you an idea of the state of the collection, but it is not a complete inventory and any problems lurking below the surface may stay undiscovered for a long while.

For manual systems many museums inventory by making a list of the objects as they are found and checking that list against the records. That list becomes an accurate record of the state of the collection at that particular time. There is, however, a lot of cross-checking of records.

You may find it easier to take one of your card catalogues and move the card for each object you find to a *found* file as you go through the collection. This method does not produce a list, so you will have to make one from the completed catalogue. I use this method and create a list in accession number order as I go along.

It is a lot easier inventorying a computerized collection. You generate a list of the objects by location, and check them off as you find them, or you can take the computer with you as you work, if it is small enough.

It is important with inventories that you end up with some list showing the state of the collection at that particular time. This list should be archived.

Certain new devices may have a profound effect on inventorying the collection in future. Using a computer with wireless capabilities one can take a laptop and use the museum's electronic catalogue to inventory the objects. Bar code readers hold a great deal of promise but they are not quite here yet. They are another device that could speed inventories. The technology is well developed, reliable, and relatively cheap. Right now they are used very much like those in a supermarket. One reads the bar code for the location; the computer then reads each object at that location. The big problem with bar codes is where to put the bars.[12] The museum field has not solved the problem of placing the bar codes directly on the object. There are safe ways to place the bar codes on most objects using paper tags. This type of technology is developing and may become a must. Finally, there are radio-activated devices that can automatically register each object in the inventory. These devices are on the market now and a few museums are using them.

An inventory requires a large commitment on the part of the museum. Make sure you can complete it before you start. One of the curses of badly registered systems is all the incomplete inventories with which one has to deal.

Access

How much of the museum's records are public documents is a question you should consider carefully. Most museums do not consider any of the registration records public information. In most cases access is restricted to only a few of the museum personnel. This practice is a sensible one. Any data made public is carefully edited before release. Remember, labels, exhibit catalogues, education programs, and similar published information are public releases of information about your catalogue.

Many museums have *portions* of their catalogue easily available to the public through a computer, or even have them on the Internet. This gives the public access without endangering the records or revealing any secrets.

If the museum catalogue is considered a public document there should be some restrictions on how it is used by the public. Locations and valuations should be privileged information. Privacy laws restrict the use of donors' names and addresses. Knowledge about the size of certain holdings may make you a juicy target for thieves.

Catalogues bring up the question of access, not only to the museum records, but the collection as well. The museum has to grant everyone equal access to the collection. This does not mean that you have to admit everyone any time they want, but you have to let people under similar circumstances have *equal* access. It is a good idea to develop a policy on access to the records and the collection. Access can be limited to legitimate research goals and a need-to-know basis. The type of examination can be restricted to certain times and methods of examination. You can forbid the handling of the object, if that is in its best interest.[13]

The examination of records can be limited to the catalogue. You can keep certain information confidential, such as the value, location, and donor's name. Government-run museums may come under so-called sunshine laws, by which they have to grant anyone access to the collection. That access does not necessarily have to be to the records. You may have to give some person a list of your Chinese teapots, but that does not mean you need to give them the whole catalogue. Even in these cases, certain knowledge, such as donors' names and the location and value of objects can be restricted, and need-to-know questions arise. Your lawyer can advise you on this.

I have placed a clause on access to the collection in the policy manuals in the appendix.

What Not to Do and When Not to Do It

A mistake people often make about a card catalogue is to confuse it with the accession records. It is tempting to type all the accession records on cards, neatly file them in some fashion, and say you have a catalogue. It is equally easy to take a card from the file and lose it or misplace it, and you have lost one of the primary records of the museum. This was true of all the problem collections with which I have dealt. If you are going to have a catalogue, keep it separate from the primary records. The catalogue gets used and will eventually have to be replaced, but the primary records should last forever.

I realize that if the museum uses the ledger as their catalogue they could eventually wear it out. I recommended in this case that the museum make a copy and use the copy instead of the original. In fact, you should copy any primary record that is going to be consulted frequently and use the copy as the working document.

Another mistake is to have a different form for each type of catalogue card. There will be a card for the main entry, another type for the room catalogue, another for the photograph. Unless you have a large printing budget and lots of people to shuffle cards, it is better to keep the number of cards to a minimum.[14] The card you use for your main entry can serve for most other cross-references. The donor, association, and lexicon cards can be typed on blank stock. One way to separate one type of card from another is to use different colored stock.

There is a trick to cataloguing. The trick is to do it right the first time. It is a common mistake when cataloguing to start off on the wrong foot, do half a job, drop it, come back later, and start again. The result is a mess. It is better to decide, at the beginning, what you really want to do, begin it carefully, and complete one section before going on to the next.

Conclusion

Cataloguing is as much a process as it is a device. The process is a constant updating of the data on the collection. This is the way we pass our knowledge on to the next set of curators. There should be a commitment on the part of the museum to updating the catalogue.

The test of any catalogue is not whether you can use it, but whether anyone else can. It should be arranged so it makes sense to anyone. Good cataloguing consists of

1. Examining every object and every record and creating an accurate description
2. Developing a usable set of categories for searches you will actually make
3. Developing a program to keep the data up to date

For paper catalogues the purpose of cataloging is to arrange your records in usable categories. It is easier to shuffle cards than objects. Museum personnel should decide what information will be needed from the catalogue and then divide the catalogue into those units. There may be other methods of cataloguing available that do not use cards. The museum must be careful not to create a catalogue monster that will eat up all the professional staff's time.

A computerized catalogue should quickly and easily provide the information you need in a usable form. Like the card catalogue, the system should be usable to any intelligent person, though he or she may have to learn the idiosyncrasies of the program first, and questions of data security arise.

Notes

1. AAM, *Peer Review Manual*, F8.

2. For a look at how librarians would handle museum cataloguing see Murtha Baca, Patricia Harping, Elisa Lanzi, Linda McRae, and Ann Whiteside, *Cataloging Cultural Objects: A Guide to Describing Cultural Objects and Their Images* (Chicago: American Library Association, 2006). The system Baca and colleagues propose is too extensive for most museums. The term "catalogue" may be correctly spelled either "catalog" or "catalogue." I prefer the latter and was convinced of its utility after two hours in a bar with a Canadian friend who explained that the term "cataloging" just could not be pronounced correctly. It seemed like a reasonable argument at the time.

3. The question of who had the first museum registration system is moot. Herodotus implies, in the fifth century BC, that there were catalogues for the collections in the several treasuries (that held historical collections) at Delphi and in Mesopotamia. This information may have been oral, but at least the priests could account for their collections and pass this knowledge on to others. Some of the information was written directly on the object. This is a method frowned on today, but one must say it would be hard to lose your catalogue. The concept of a collection ledger was developed in Hellenistic times (350–0 BC). There are collection ledgers referred to for the Renaissance collections. For a survey see Geoffrey D. Lewis, "Collections, Collectors and Museums: A Brief World Survey," in John M. A. Thompson, et al, eds. *Manual of Curatorship: A Guide to Museum Practice* (London: Butterworths, 1984).

4. Compare Kitty Longstreth-Brown, "Documentation: Manual Systems," in Buck and Gilmore, *New Museum Registration Methods*, 1–12, and Suzanne Quigley, "Documentation: Computerized Systems," in Buck and Gilmore, *New Museum Registration Methods*, 17–37.

5. James R. Blackaby, Patricia Greeno, et al, *The Revised Nomenclature for Museum Cataloging: A Revised and Expanded Version of Robert G. Chenhall's System for Classifying Man-Made Objects.* Revised and expanded by James R. Blackaby, Patricia Greeno, and the Nomenclature Committee (Nashville: AASLH, 1988). It is still in print. It is interesting, but Chenhall's work, originally meant to aid in the computerization of collections, has proved even more useful with manual records.

6. A taxonomy is the classification of a something into a natural arrangement. The list itself is a taxis. "Lexicon," "nomenclature," and "dictionary" are more or less interchangeable terms.

7. Elisa Lanzi, et al., *Introduction to Vocabularies: Enhancing Access to Cultural Heritage Information* (Los Angeles: J. Paul Getty Trust, 1998).

8. The reason for placing the name of the museum at the bottom of the card is that it will identify the museum, while the important information is at the top.

9. Virginia Pointer, "Photography," in Buck and Gilmore, *New Museum Registration Methods*, 95–102.

10. Jill Marie Koelling, *Digital Imaging: A Practical Approach* (Walnut Creek, CA: AltaMira Press, 2004); Christie Stephenson and Patricia McClung, eds., *Delivering*

Digital Images: Cultural Heritage Resources for Education (Los Angeles: The Getty Institute, 1998).

11. Suzanne Cowan, "Inventory," in Buck and Gilmore, *New Museum Registration Methods*, 117–119.

12. Catherine Zwiesler, "Barcoding," *Spectra* 23, no. 1 (Fall 1995), 18–20, discusses use of bar codes at the National Museum of Natural History. *Spectra* was the newsletter of the Museum Computer Network. Gabor R. Racz, "Improving Collection Maintenance through Innovation: Bar-Code Labeling to Track Specimens in the Processing Stream," *Collections* 1, no. 3 (February 2005), 227–241.

13. Access to the museum collection and the records has not been a very big issue up until recently. It is the kind of situation people worry about before it happens. However, it is good to be prepared. Malaro, *Primer*, 293–294.

14. As an example, James Blackaby et al., *Managing Historic Data, Special Report #3*, (Nashville: AASLH, 1989), shows *seven* different cards with eight sides. For my typical museum of 10,000 objects, this would be 70,000 cards, more than 35 drawers!

CHAPTER SEVEN

Loans

Unless the exhibits and the collection are very static, a museum will lend and borrow objects. The museum will find that its collection is never complete enough to make up every exhibit. It is a good museum practice and good public relations to have exhibits of items from the community. Other museums and organizations will want to tap your resources. Items are often lent or borrowed for purposes of study or conservation. The sophisticated handling of loans is part of the registration process. Like any other part of the registration process, the museum should decide how deeply it wants to get into loans and create the policy to do this, and the procedures will develop out of this.[1]

Loan Policy

Many problems with loans will never occur if the museum has a strong policy on loans. The policy should assure that

- The loan furthers the purpose of the museum. If your statement of purpose declares that the museum wishes "to encourage the preservation and study of Hero County history," then the loan should do just that.
- The object will be cared for properly while on loan.
- The registration system can track the object over the whole period of the loan even if that is several years!

Every loan should be tested against these conditions. There are examples of such policies in appendices B and C.

There is something of a difference between things a museum borrows and things it lends, so we are going to discuss these separately. As in any other contractual relationship between a museum and second parties, the loan policies, the loan form, and the types of liability assumed should be gone over carefully with a lawyer before the museum becomes involved in loans.

Loans from the Museum

When a museum lends items out from its collection it is very simple. The museum owns the object lent and can set its own conditions. The museum can have absolute control over how the object is used. Criteria for conditions for loans from the museum are listed below and in appendix A-9.

Loans to the Museum

You are on slightly different ground when you borrow something than when you lend. When you lend, the object involved is your property, and you can set the conditions. When you borrow it is not your property, and you must follow the owner's wishes, and you take on a liability. You are obligated to return the loan in the same condition in which you received it. You are responsible for it as long as you have it. If the owner does not show up to reclaim it, you are still responsible for it. If the lender appears thirty-three years later, as happened to me once, you are still responsible. Therefore, it is a very good idea to borrow only for specific purposes, such as display, and for a specific time period, and return things as soon as possible.

On a loan to the museum you must usually provide the protection, shipping costs, and insurance. Most museums agree to protect the item as if it were their own and to carry fine arts insurance. The owner may want to set other conditions, and these should be stated on the form. Criteria for conditions for a loan to the museum are below and in appendix A-10.

Whose Loan Procedures Will Apply?

As a practical matter there should only be one loan agreement on a loan. On loans between museums, the lending institution will have the upper hand, and it will almost always be its procedure and forms. This can be pretty tricky when the museums vary widely in operating procedures. On third-party loans, such as loans for traveling exhibits, the policies of the originating museum will probably apply. Your loan form for loans to your museum is for people who normally do not have their own form, such as individuals and private companies.

Conditions of Loans

The general conditions affecting every loan should be printed on the loan form and discussed with the other parties. If there will be special conditions that are not on the loan form, these should then be made a written part of the loan documents. Before the object is moved the loan form should be signed by all parties.

Whether the loan is from or to the museum certain conditions arise which should be accounted for in the museum's policy and loan arrangements.

What Is Actually Being Borrowed?

The loan form should state exactly what is being borrowed listing every item. On loans from your museum your accession records are very handy, as you can place the accession number and a description from your records on the loan form. On loans to the museum you may have to go to the lending person or agency and make an exact description of what is borrowed and a condition report.

The description of the object should be good enough to identify it in court. The museum's description of its own objects should do that. If the description of a borrowed item is not good enough, you will have to make a new one. When borrowing from a private person you should go over the description and make sure the lender agrees with your description, particularly of condition.

The Exact Purpose of the Loan

The purpose of the loan should be stated on the form. If you lend a copper pot for exhibit you do not want to see it used for cooking. It is best for the museum to have a policy on limiting loans to certain specific purposes. Many museums simplify the process by developing a policy that they will only borrow objects for exhibit in the museum, and only lend objects to other museums for the same purpose. Museums with a local following may find it expedient to lend to community organizations that are able to take care of the object. In addition, there should be some way to lend objects for conservation or study.

How the Object Is to Be Cared For and Handled While on Loan

It is very important to have an understanding of exactly how the object is to be handled while on exhibit. That means if it is to be exhibited only, how much, if any, access will anyone have to it during the loan? But also what happens to it before it reaches its final destination? Is the janitor going to unpack it or the curator? Where it is going to be stored en route? Who is going to handle it while on exhibit and how? Who is going to pack it when the loan period is up? These are typical but important considerations.

Normally, the borrowers' care of the object is limited to simple dusting, although even that may not be allowed for certain objects. The other party should notify the lender of any change in the condition of the object, and be forbidden to make repairs in the case of damage. How the object is to be cased, lighted, protected, and other environmental concerns are all conditions that should be agreed upon in advance.

If the object requires special handling, should not be in harsh light, must be in controlled humidity, needs special security, etc., these conditions should be gone over step by step with the borrower before the loan is made. It is a good idea to go over all the provisions of the loan before the loan form is signed. One thing you should know is if the donors want their name advertised in another location.

An Assessment of the Object's Condition and Ability to Travel and Withstand the Conditions It Will Be Under during the Loan

Any details of condition should be noted before the object is sent out. The condition should be the same when it is brought back. You should have a condition report (see appendix A) on each object in the loan, whether from or to the museum, and have both parties agree on the statements on this form. You may need two condition reports or have to update the original: once when the object is lent, and once when it is returned. If you are borrowing an object, and there is no condition report by the lender, then that should be noted. You should demand that you be able to make a condition report at the time of the receipt, and that this be the condition of record. Otherwise, the borrower may claim you caused old damage.

Condition reports should not only be made out when the object is loaned, but whenever it is examined. Ideally, there should be at least one condition report on each object in the collection. As the object is monitored you can amend the form.

The condition of the building that houses the object is also a consideration. Many museums have a facility report that they use for loans to other agencies. There is a standard form developed by the Registrars Committee of

AAM.[2] Filling in the facilities report is a time-consuming thing, but only has to be done once and then can be used with any other loan.

An object may be in good enough condition to be exhibited in one place, but in too fragile a condition to be exhibited in another. An assessment of the object's ability to travel is an important part of the loan process. If the other party has really got to have this object, it is an occasional practice for them to pay for the conservation necessary (or at least share the cost) to have the object travel.

Method of Packing or Crating

How the object is to be packed for shipping, and who will do it, are important questions. For many objects, packing as for a typical move of household goods is not good enough, and for most objects specialized packing or crating will usually be required and even climate control may be necessary. Unpacking is a concern at both ends of the deal, when it goes out and when it comes back. How this is done and who will pack and unpack should be part of the loan agreement.

Method of Transporting the Object
and Who Is Responsible for the Shipment

There is a museum in western Pennsylvania where board members were expected to move objects. They once had a provision that to become a board member you had to have a pickup truck. That may work with agricultural equipment but it will not work in most museums.

Make sure that both borrower and lender know how the object is to be transferred and know who is responsible for the transfer. Is it going to be the curator, a courier, a trucking company, a local moving company, or an expert in transporting fine arts? The borrower is usually responsible for making the arrangements and paying for the move. These conditions should be approved by every party. When lending objects make sure the borrower will move the object with sufficient care, equipment, and personnel *both* ways.

The problem you sometimes run into in loans is where the other party will be located at the end of the loan term. If you borrow an object from a lender who is located ten miles away then the costs and problems of the move are very clear. But what happens if that same person moves 3,000 miles away during the loan period? This situation does not just apply to individuals but can happen to museums as well. It is best to specify that the costs of the move only apply to shipment to the address on the loan form.

What happens if the owners sell or transfer the property while it is on loan is also a consideration. They should notify you in writing if this occurs. You should normally not return an object to anyone but the person who signed the loan form as the owner. If it is transferred, it is the owner's responsibility to provide proof of the transfer, not the museum's.

Museums often have problems of not being able to return an object when the loan period is up. The owner, for one reason or another, is not available to take it back. The museum should require that, if it cannot return the object because the owner cannot receive it, then the museum can exercise a lower standard of care, or even charge rent. In some states it is possible that the object could eventually become the museum's property. Most museums, however, may be required to keep the property indefinitely until a legitimate owner is ready to receive it. In the case of the death of the owner the museum may have to keep the object until the estate is settled. This can run to years.

All the Locations in Which the Loan Will Be

The exact route the object is to taken to its final destination, and where it will rest en route, should be agreed upon. I once had a very valuable object left untended in the middle of a busy mall by what I thought was a responsible borrower. It was lucky that I happened along to rescue it.

It is best if the borrower keeps the object in his or her possession and returns it to the museum when the term of the loan is completed. Sometimes there is a reason to lend it to a third party. A good example would be a museum making up a traveling exhibition from the collections of several museums.

The Exact Dates of the Loan Period, Wall to Wall

The date of the loan period should include the date the agreement is made, the date the object is to be picked up, the dates of the exhibit (if the object is lent for that purpose), and the date it is to be returned. There should never be any confusion about loan dates.

Almost all loans are made "wall to wall." That means the borrower is responsible for the object from the time it is first handled to prepare it to be moved until it is returned to that same place, or one mutually agreeable to both parties. That means the borrower's responsibility begins once anyone lays his or her hand on it while it is still in the owner's building.

There are "door-to-door" agreements, in which the borrower is only responsible for the object after it leaves the lender's door, until it is returned there. These are not popular anymore, as the preparation of the object for transport is now considered part of the loan process. If you do not specify that the loan is wall to wall then the loan would probably be considered door to door.

The loan should have definite time limits. A loan to the museum should not continue for a long period of time; a year is long enough and three years are about the maximum. Occasionally, museums borrow for longer periods of time. One should hesitate to request an unusually long time period, but sometimes there is a good reason: it may be the only way some rare item can be exhibited, or the owner may not have clear title just yet. These long-term loans should be for a period of a year, renewable from year to year. This practice will remind both parties that it is still a loan, and will remind you to keep up your fine arts insurance. The number of these long-term loans should be kept to a minimum.

The Value of Each Object in the Loan

The value of the object is a very complicated thing when insurance is involved. If you have a damaged object that is worth $1,000 and the repairs cost $1,500, who is responsible for the difference? Again, the insurance company may pay the $1,000 and then take the object for its salvage value. The owners may only get $800 or so if they keep the object. What happens if one of a set gets destroyed? Overvaluing an object to take care of some of this may not work as the insurance company usually will only insure a "fair market value." Emotional value is usually not insurable. The museum should agree that it is only responsible for the declared value and make sure that value is reasonable for the object.

Each object in the loan should have its own value. This is important as damage or theft to the whole loan will practically never come up, but damage to a single piece will be an occasional occurrence. Sometimes the museum will have exhibits of items collected from the community, such as a senior citizens art fair. It may be impossible to evaluate each object, but you can give a range of values, $X to $XXX, that will cover the whole loan.

The museum should be careful about offering to place a value on objects lent to it. This may place the museum in the position of evaluating the object for market. If something happens and the value is incorrect it may place the museum in a bad legal position. The owner might claim damages. If there is a problem with this then you may have to hire an appraiser. Who pays for this is an interesting question.

The Type and Nature of the Insurance
and Who Is Responsible for Paying for It

You need to have a fine arts policy. First of all, you are dealing with people who work with museums. It is cheaper than casualty insurance, and is better for the time the accession is in transit. Normal casualty insurance will not work as it is interested only in salvage value.

The usual practice is for the borrower to be responsible for the insurance. It is important to have proof of insurance. There is a form any insurance agent should be able to produce called a "certificate of insurance." When borrowing make sure that the insurance is not due to expire while the object is on loan. The expiration date will usually be on the certificate of insurance. A 120-day cancellation clause is a useful thing on these certificates of insurance. In the case of objects of small value, where the borrower is well known, the museum may waive the demand for insurance. The lender really does not want the money; they want the object back in the same condition it was in when you borrowed it.

The Name and Signature of the Person Actually Responsible for the Loan

If the person borrowing the object represents the organization, he or she should be responsible enough to place his or her organization under the obligation of caring for the object.

The person who signs for the loan should be a person who is really responsible for it, not the person who is picking it up. These are often two different people. The person who picks up the object should also sign, but may not be the responsible person.

This can be one of the tricky parts of loan arrangements. The organization responsible for the object may not be located at the museum, or even be in the same city (or state) as the exhibiting organization. It is important to get the name of a responsible person, and the exact address of everyone involved. If there is a parent organization, it might be a good idea to find out if it knows that its satellite museum is borrowing the object. Museums may have different street addresses for the offices, the exhibit hall, and the shipping dock. Get them all.

Request for the Return of the Loan Before the Loan Period Is Up

It is not unknown for an owner to request the return of the object before the loan period is up. That may leave a big hole in your exhibit. Common practice is to allow this, but to require a thirty- or sixty-day notice before exercising this right. It is customary to have the person requesting the early return of the loan pay the packing and shipping fees.

Control of Intellectual Property

The intellectual property of the museum consists of such things as the images of the objects in the collection, the content and appearance of documents, the content and methods of education programs, publications, etc. If the appearance of the buildings or site of the museum is part of the "signature" or "brand" of the museum, that, too, is intellectual property. Museums were pretty careless with their intellectual property rights until recently. With the advent of sophisticated communication devices this intellectual property suddenly has a real value to the museum. Steps should be made to protect it, particularly while on loan.

Although the image or design of the object itself may be in the public domain, a photographic or electronic image of it may be copyrighted as will a reproduction of the object itself. Museums should control who takes these images or makes copies and what purpose they are used for. Before you allow anyone to photograph or otherwise copy anything in the museum, you should restrict the use of it to a certain time period, and to certain uses ("A one-time use in a book on left-handed monkey wrenches"). While the object is on loan to another institution, you may want to restrict the right to photograph the object to only record-keeping purposes, or for a catalogue.

The new forms of electronic imagery are so sophisticated that any use has to be carefully circumscribed or you can lose all control over the image of an object in your collection. This has applied mainly to artwork in the past, but one should guard all intellectual property. I have clauses in my loan forms that restrict use of images to record shots and a one-time use in a catalogue.

Amending the Loan Agreement

You should guard against oral amendments to the loan agreement. It is too easy to have a misunderstanding. There should be a clause that the agreement may only be amended in writing and must be signed by both parties.

Loan Numbers and a Loan Register

Museums that borrow a lot of material often keep a loan register and assign numbers to each borrowed item. This is a good idea if you are mounting four or six large loan exhibits a year or have a large turnover in loans. Loan registers are normally kept only for loans to the museum. You already have a record of your own objects, and the loan register gives you control over all the objects in the museum that are not part of your collection. Some museums can also keep a register of objects loaned from the museum, but I do not think that is necessary, unless you have an inordinate number of loans. Loan numbers were discussed in chapter 3, but are only assigned to the items you borrow; your own objects have accession numbers. A loan register might look like the example in the appendix. The loan register should be checked periodically and the status of all loans cleared. At the end of the year, the register and all loans should be up to date and the status of all loans reported to the board.

I am only suggesting a loan register, as it is an excellent device to keep track of loans, if you have a number of them during the year. I would doubt it would be necessary if you make fewer than five or so such transactions a year. Whether a loan register would be helpful depends on the staff and the time you have available. Keeping all the documents on current loans in a file is another way of tracking them.

Unless you have some way of entering objects on loan to the museum into your computer a loan register may be necessary with that device as well. If the museum borrows only a few objects a year, I would think that creating a computer record on them is a lot of work. If you have a large number of loans to the museum, you may find such a record necessary. There are things called "flags" in many computer programs. These allow you to tag certain records with a number or letter. Flagging objects is a good way of tracking all loans from the museum.

Conservation Loans

Museums often lend or borrow things for conservation or identification. These transactions are handled pretty much the same as any other loan. When the museum lends out an object to be conserved, the administration should have a pretty good idea what the conservator is going to do with it. The conservator should look at the object before borrowing it and then state in writing what he or she proposes to do. If this is impossible, the object is sent to the conservator for examination first. The conservator will then report back on the proposed treatment. If that is agreeable, the recommendation is made part of the loan form. The loan agreement should be loose enough to allow the conservator some room to work if the conservator runs into problems and tight enough to prevent him or her from doing more than the museum staff wishes. The time limits have to be somewhat looser on these loans as the conservator will often run into problems, and you do not want to hurry the conservator, but there should be a finite time limit. Loans can always be extended.

The museum or its staff will sometimes do conservation work for outsiders. When that is done, the transaction becomes a business deal and not a museum function. The museum should have the protections that any business has, particularly liability coverage. One of the ways to justify the cost of a conservation laboratory is the ability to use the excess capacity of the lab for outside work. In these instances, the museum should be as strict on its procedure on the items it takes in as if it were borrowing any other item.

Deposit or "Drop-Off" Loans

If someone leaves an object at the museum, even without the knowledge or permission of the museum, that object is very likely the museum's responsibility until it is returned. There are also loans pending gift, or similar temporary loans. For these reasons, it is best to have a policy about what is to be received at the museum. This is especially important with volunteer-run museums, where there may be a large number of people working at the reception area of the museum over the course of the year. It might be best to have a simple statement such as the example placed where every volunteer can see it:

> If anyone brings in an object with the offer to donate, sell, or lend it to the Hero County Historical Society, the object may not be accepted or left at the museum without the permission of Mrs. Supreme Optimist, 728-2208, or Mrs. Usually V. Negative, 266-4500. If they are not available, inform the potential donor that the Society may be interested in their object, but that you may not receive it, and that the potential donor should get in touch with either of those persons.

If permission is granted, then the proper form can be signed, so that both parties know their responsibilities.

In instances such as this, the museum may find it useful to have a "deposit" form that allows prospective donors to temporarily leave items at the museum while awaiting action. A deposit form allows museums to keep the object for a short period of time, pending the preparation of other forms, but does not obligate them as deeply as a loan form or gift agreement might. A sample deposit form is appendix A-11.

People will often bring things to the museum for identification. It is a good practice to have a policy on this. I recommend not doing it at all. If the museum accepts an object for identification it is a loan just as much as any other loan. It should be treated accordingly. If the museum receives no real benefit from the loan, there is a question whether it should be accepted at all. Some museums have a separate form for identification or conservation loans, but I do not think it is necessary.

There is a small historical society to which someone once offered to give twenty-five thousand sea shells (all different), weighing 2½ tons. Only chance kept the shells from being left. A procedure such as outlined above can prevent embarrassment.

Existing Long-Term Loans

There is no such thing as a permanent loan; it is either a loan or it is not. Lawyers have a fascinating language. I used to play bridge with two of them and asked them to research our legal liabilities with regard to loans. One came up with the fact that a loan was a "gratuitous bailment without the right of survivorship." I liked that. Both agreed that a loan never becomes the museum's property, no matter how long it is kept, though that situation has been changed in certain states. As I pointed out, there may be a good reason to take in a long-term loan, but never kid yourself that it is yours. It is best to have such loans on a one- or two-year basis, and then neither party will forget the status of the property.

Laws vary widely, and there may be some way of claiming legal title. Almost half the states have passed laws that allow the museum to acquire title to permanent loans.

For everyone else, acquiring title to long-term loans is difficult, at best, and is always subject to question if the owner or heirs appear. In one case with which I am familiar, the heirs showed up more than ninety years later. Only the fact that there were twenty heirs and they could not agree on who got the objects kept the items in the museum. Even under such circumstances, such objects are not the museum's, nor will they ever be, under the present laws of that state.[3]

The best method of clearing such loans is to attempt to track down the original lenders or their heirs and to try to get them to donate the objects or to claim them. That is a time-consuming and unpleasant task, but it may be necessary. When you try to clear up long-term loans, you often risk losing a valuable object, but that is better than offering free storage.

What Not to Do And When Not to Do It

Do not fail to get everything in writing. Loans are usually made to people with whom the museum is acquainted. There is a tendency to be a bit careless on procedure when the object has no great value or the deal is between friends. If you have a loan procedure, it is a good idea to stick to it. If any questions come up, you will have the details in writing.

Many things about loans that should not be done fall into the curatorial area rather than the area of registration, and so are outside the scope of this book. The person making the loan must ensure that the object will be taken care of when it is out of the museum and that the loan will not bring discredit to the museum. For that reason, I am always leery of loans for promotional purposes. You never know, if you lend a carriage to an automobile dealer for promotion, that you will not see it prominently displayed in all the media with a caption, "Look at this stupid, creaky old carriage that we got from the musty old historical society. Why drive this when you can drive a Total?"[4]

It is wise to make sure that any prospective borrowers who are unknown to you are actually who they say they are and really represent the organization they claim to represent. We usually insist that the borrowers write to us on the organizations' stationary, stating what they want to borrow and how they intend to display it.

Loans to the museum tend to be carefully made and cared for until the exhibit is over, and then the pressure is off. You may get a little careless then. That loan is your baby until the owner has it in hand and is satisfied with its condition. Do not relax your care a minute.

When a museum borrows or lends an object, it places its reputation on the line. A carefully thought-out loan procedure will prevent most problems. Remember, in 999 cases out of 1,000, things go well. The one time when there is a problem is the one that causes all the trouble. The loan policy of the museum should be such that it handles the 999 cases well and has all its homework done for the one problem case.

Notes

1. Malaro, *Primer*, 156–234, has an extensive discussion of the legal aspects of loans; Phelan, *Museum Law*, 107–108, has a more limited discussion of loans but in her *Museum Law*, 273–277, there is an extensive discussion from the lawyer's viewpoint. Sally Freitag and Cherie Summers, "Loans," in Buck and Gilmore, *New Museum Registration Methods*, 177–188 and *passim*. AAM Registrars Committee, Professional Practices Subcommittee, "Loan Survey Report," May 1990, reported some rather interesting things. One was that 21 percent of history museums did not have a loan policy. I doubt things have changed much.

2. AAM Registrars Committee, *Standard Facility Report*, Professional Practice Series, AAM Technical Service (Washington, DC: AAM, 1989).

3. Malaro, *Primer*, 165–167, 195–293, and 178–179 has an excellent discussion of "permanent loans"; see also Ildiko DeAngelis, "Old Loans," in Buck and Gilmore, *New Museum Registration Methods*, 281–288; an old work, that may be hard to find, but which is quite valuable, is Anita Manning, "Converting Loans to Gifts," *AASLH Technical Leaflet #94* (Nashville: AASLH, 1977); Phelan, *Museum Law*, 108, notes that there are two types of gratuitous bailments depending on the "benefit" one gets from the loan.

4. Be aware that you may be creating a precedent when you lend objects to commercial or noneducational agencies which may force you to lend museum items to agencies or for purposes which you would rather not; Malaro, *Primer*, 174–175. But Malaro does not know of a single instance where this has occurred. She just warns you that the possibility exists.

CHAPTER EIGHT

~

Computers

"If you think you are having problems with your registration system now—just wait until you get a computer."

—Modern folk saying

Computers are now part of the modern world culture as much as a fountain pen was fifty years ago. They give us a tool that can create, edit, sort, and otherwise manipulate data far beyond what any human can do. A computer can do a lot of good things for your registration system, but it is just a machine, and like any other machine, you have to have the right one for the job.[1]

I am going to suggest an approach to computers that will fit the small museum. I am going to assume that the reader knows enough about computers to make intelligent choices, or can acquire this knowledge. One cannot be too specific in this chapter as the technology changes so quickly that if I get too technical the advice will be obsolete before this is published.

A collections management program should be able to do the following things:

- Store data in a useful format
- Edit data
- Delete data
- Access the data in some useful form including making "string searches," that is, all the records where certain words appear in any combination, such as "fan back" and "Windsor"

- Sort data in various ways but particularly in what is called a "dictionary sort," that is, in strict alphabetical and numerical order
- Edit and write reports to paper or screen

First Steps

A lot of the failures in using computers result from poor planning. You have to know what you really need before you buy anything. The first thing you should do is make a needs assessment of your museum. The people involved in the collection should get together and develop a list of things they would like to get from the registration system. An analysis of actual searches for information is useful. In looking at these you begin to understand where you go to look for information and what you look for. A step-by-step analysis of the most common processes, such as accessioning, loans, catalogue searches for exhibits, updating catalogues, donor requests, inventories, etc., are very useful. These lists show you who needs to know what, how much they need to know, in what form, and how often the information is needed. Just as importantly, they show you what information you do not need. An example of a simple analysis of a record search is shown in figure 16.

A look at your policies and procedures is in order. Do your current records reflect museum policy? An electronic data bank will certainly affect policy. You may no longer need all the paper forms you used to have. How you will create a permanent record is important. Who has access to the data bank is an essential question so you will need new security procedures.

Then you are ready to start making up a list of fields you want to include. A field is a discrete piece of information, such as the accession number. You can be quite generous to yourself when first making up this list of fields. Put in every one you think you will need. The list can (and certainly will) be cut down later. Start thinking about what the field will contain. Should it be only text? Should it be only numbers? How long should it be? These decisions need only be general ideas at this stage as the type of software you select will have a great deal of bearing on the number and makeup of the fields. A reduced list of the fields, recommended by the Common Agenda Data Bases Task Force, is in chapter 4, but see the section on the number of fields below.

The most important thing to consider is that the information you want to get out of the system is the information you must put in. If you are going to require information that is not presently in your records then you must start thinking about how you are going to transfer it for your new system. For instance, if you do not now track condition, how are you going to find this data

EXAMPLE OF THE ANALYSIS OF A TYPICAL CARD CATALOGUE FILE SEARCH
Subject of search: "Typical tools on a cabinetmakers workbench."

Actions:	Analysis:
Make a list of the tools needed: a bench; types of planes, braces, bits, saws, hammers, clamps, rulers, squares, etc. Sometimes this is done mentally.	Chenhall has a classification for this that would pull all these up at once.
Search catalogue for requisite cards. Search main entry catalogue. Look through entire tool catalogue. Remove cards as potential objects are found	The ability to flag, or mark, particular records would be useful so that after the initial search we can find these records again.
List objects by name, number and location.	The program must be able to generate a report for this purpose.
Search storage for objects.	How are we going to mark location? Should objects "live" at one spot? Shelf lists would be useful.
Return cards to file.	
Assemble objects in dummy exhibit. Select ones for use.	The flag system has to allow for the objects to be either placed on exhibit or returned to their proper place in storage. If there is need to borrow objects for the exhibit we need ability to account for this.
Set up exhibit.	We need to be able to easily extract information for labels. We need to be able to easily extract donor names for labels. We need to know if there are restrictions on identifying donors. If we are going to track the history of the movement of the object, then we need a record of locations including the exhibit. Need ability to track objects while on exhibit.
Orient interpreters, write hand-out literature.	Need the ability to pull up information for training purposes. It would be useful to be able to transport catalogue information for labels and training guides.
Take down exhibit.	Need to track objects back to storage.

Figure 16: Needs Analysis. There is no particular format for this form. It is important that it covers your present situation and your future needs.

and put it in your system? Conversely, if you never look at the date of acquisition, why put it in?

Information That Is Actually Used

When you first see a museum computer system there is often a fascinating variety of screens and data fields. This is all very interesting, but the experience of the museum field is that the more screens and data fields you have the more difficult it is to enter data into the data bank and access information afterwards. You may want a fancy system, but what you really need is a simple system that fits on one or two screens and that will lead you quickly and easily to either the object or the paper record.

The Number of Fields

In its day, the lowly catalogue card was a very effective data storage device. You could only get so much data on it so its small size promoted efficient use of data. In their mass the cards were almost impossible to use effectively, and stored enormous amounts of redundant data but had a brute efficiency for storing essential data.[2]

When computers first began to have a large impact on the museum field (late 1960s and 1970s) a favorite input/output device was also a card, a punch card, though some data was stored on tape. Each card held about 80 bits of data, though techniques were developed to have more on a card or more than one card in a record. Rather than put every card through the machine every time you wanted to address the computer, or get all your data reels out, systems were developed to classify the terminology, an index as it were, so that you only had to put a drawer or two of cards through the machine instead of every card in the file. This may seem hopelessly slow and clumsy by today's technology, but it was incredibly fast by the standards then.

In the absence of adequate indices one had lots of fields. Curators used to get together and discuss the number of fields they had and try to top each other: "You have 110 fields? Wow, I have 220." As computers got bigger and faster the number of fields diminished.

Because computers were so slow by today's standards, the classification systems perpetuated the idea that museum registration systems had to be able to be broken down into families, even when we advanced beyond punch cards. The system adapted by the history museum field was Robert G. Chenhall's *Nomenclature.*[3]

As we have discussed above, until Chenhall there was no single classification system for the history museum field. His system gave us a way of making the English language act like a systematic language. Chenhall's system was widely adopted by the history museum field, and to a lesser extent by the art and anthropology field.

Though originally intended for computerized collections, the Chenhall system worked well with paper records. In fact, the naming convention, with the noun first followed by the modifier, provided a good sorting method if not a classification system. For many museums Chenhall proved more valuable for the naming conventions than it ever was for its classification system.

His classification system was more useful in large museums with varied collections though it still has uses in the smallest collection.

Later on there were "authority lists." These were mainly developed by the art museum world of which the *Art and Architecture Thesaurus* is the best known and most widely adopted by the museum field. Rather than provide a single term for each object, these lists provided almost every term, though one term usually could be designated as "preferred." These authority lists were so large, hard to administer, and relatively expensive that they were mainly adopted by large museums.

In the 1990s the PC became large enough, fast enough, and cheap enough so that any museum could afford one. Computers superceded almost all manual systems of registration. A number of museums developed their own electronic registration system with varying success. Today most museums of any size have at least some of their collection in a computerized form. We went back to lots of fields.

What has all this got to do with anything? The computers used by the early systems were so small that a collection record had to be small and efficient. Today, the record can be almost any size, but the people remain the same. I have an ideal size for a museum collection when discussing abstracts. It is 10,000 objects. If you have 50 fields in my ideal-sized museum then you have 500,000 blank spaces in your system that need to be filled with data. If you have 100 fields you have the potential of a million pieces of data for your collection. Do you need that much data? Probably not. I have seen two relatively new data management systems lately. One has over 250 fields and the other must have more, though, being modular, it is hard to tell, but it has at least 200 fields or 2.5 million and 2 million total datum fields respectively in each of these collections that have to be addressed.

I challenge you to count the number of fields in your museum's system and then multiply it by the size of your collection. You will be surprised.

All the Fields You Will Ever Need
I think you can put most information in the description and use the computer for what it does best, make its own classification system. I think almost all museums can get along with fifteen or twenty fields. For my ten-thousand-object collection that is 150,000 to 200,000 potential entries; that is surely enough and is more than many small museums can handle.

If you analyze a typical search for useful information in your present system you will find that you are using only ten or fifteen pieces of data. You seldom have to know if it is painted blue or has astragal ends. What you usually look for is very simple and very specific.

This is the information asked for in most searches of a museum catalogue:

- Accession number
- Title of object ("genus" and "species")
- Classification (*Nomenclature*)
- How acquired (gift, purchase, etc.)
- Source (donor, from whom purchased, etc.)
- Location
- Material
- Size
- Place of origin
- Maker
- Date (of manufacture)
- Description
- Association
- Image
- Comment
- Value
- Flag

This record of seventeen fields contains most of the information that you will ever need. With some clever manipulation you can get all of these fields on one screen. A record of this length is capable of supporting sophisticated questions such as the location of all silver tea sets with gadrooning made in Boston before 1810 by specific makers.

Accession Number
The numbering field is very important as that ties the object to the records. If you have two or more numbering systems an extra field or fields for the other numbering systems is useful. Using these extra number fields you can utilize some of the old numbering systems when necessary. The computer can also show the relationship between the several numbering systems.

Title and Classification
As we have discussed, these fields are used to identify and classify the object. For reasons of clarity and ease of entry, you need a separate field for the title and the classification. If you do not have a large collection you might be able to skip the classification field.

How Acquired

Using this field you can separate out the donations from the purchases and other means of acquisition. If you have long-term loans and deaccessions this field will help identify them. The field need only be one letter long, as an example, L for "loan." Some museums call this the "status" field.

Source

The source field is a useful field that is used constantly in museums with any number of donations. In the case of purchases, the contributor of the funds is entered, rather than from whom purchased. I would recommend listing the vendors in the "Comments" field as you seldom need to know who they are.

Location

The best way to indicate location in a computer is to have the object "live" at one location, and only track it when it is moved. This is discussed in chapter 6 on cataloguing.

Material

The effectiveness of the material field depends on what the material is. When the object is made mainly of one material, such as glass, silver, tin, or wrought iron, then you will find it a useful way to find or classify certain objects. When there are many materials, such as an automobile or chair made of seven different woods, the field will be nearly useless for creating a class, but very useful for identification. It is better to be specific in terminology: "maple" instead of "wood."

Size

The size field is a lot more useful in a computer than it is in a paper catalogue. If you have a separate field for width, height, depth, or diameter you can extract the number of running feet objects slated for an exhibit will need or the cubic volume of the collection. If the size field is to be used in this fashion the dimensions have to be entered decimally. Size fields can be configured to give either inch/foot or metric measurements, and can convert one automatically to the other.

Place of Origin

Where the object originated is of great importance as that often influences the style, material, method of construction, or even how the object was used. It is better to be specific: "Boston" rather than "New England." In some collections, the place of use will be important and you may need a separate field for that as well.

Maker

The "Maker" field is actually the "Creator" field. You should list the artist, engraver, craftsman, manufacturer, printer as well as publisher, and any other person or entity that had a hand in the creation of the object. If the maker is a school or group (Shakers, U.S. Navy, etc.), that should be indicated here.

Date of Manufacture

The date of manufacture is very important, but this is where you have to insist on rigid standards. The computer cannot tell the difference between "ca. 1840," "c. 1840," "about 1840," and "1835–1845." You have to pick one method. I do not like the use of around (ca.) in a computer data bank as it is vague and difficult to access or sort. I prefer to use a range of dates, such as "1770–1800" for either "later 18th century" or "ca. 1784." In buying or implementing software see how well the program handles a range of dates. You may need two fields for a beginning and ending date.

Description

The description will be a very useful thing if you are capable of entering all that data. If you have a description field make sure that your program will search the description field for the data you need. You need to be able to perform "string searches" that allow you to search for relationships such as all the records that contain the words "bow back" and "Windsor." In that fashion you can find all the Windsor chairs with bow backs without having a style field. Instead of a separate field for such things as user or color, include them in the description. This cuts down the number of fields and gives you a great deal of flexibility in searches. See chapter 6 on cataloguing.

Association

The computer makes it easier to search for an association of an object with a person, place, or event than a card catalogue. It is important that your program can make "string searches" for useful data, such as the relationship of George Washington with the Whiskey Rebellion. If you are using a computer, you will have to have fairly strict rules on how this information is to be entered if you expect to make any kind of search of this field. This is a time-consuming field to create, but once it is done, you will use it more than any other.

Image

If you use a digital image as part of the registration program then you need an image field. If you have it as a separate image file then you have to indicate in the registration program that you have an image.

Comment

A "comment" field is also useful for all that information that is not included in other fields.

Value

Some museums place a value on each object in the collection. You can manipulate this value. You can get a total value for the collection or a portion of it, you could upgrade the value if prices rise, or you could get a value for just a part of the collection. You could find out what your risk is in certain areas ("the total value of the objects stored in room 101"). It could give you a total on a certain class of objects, such as all the silver. Some programs will even round off these values when you raise them. If you do not place a value on the collection then you can eliminate this field.

Flag

A flag field is useful. You can "flag" certain groups of objects that are otherwise unrelated. For instance, you can "flag" a group of unrelated objects that are to be loaned to another museum and call up their records anytime by their flag. This saves calling up each record individually. It can be only two letters wide and that will give you a range of flags from $a–zz$ and 00–99.

Condition

I have not included a condition field in the ones above, but it would be a useful field if you can track it. Using a simplified ranking method you can establish lists of objects in priority of their need for conservation. You can use this to track condition. A simple system using only one letter space is

"1" indicates the condition "Urgent." The object needs immediate care.

"2" indicates the condition "Serious but Not Urgent." The safety of the object is in jeopardy and its condition will become urgent if not conserved.

"3" indicates the condition "Requires Treatment." If stored properly the treatment may be delayed.

"4" indicates the condition "exhibitable." Should be exhibitable if handled carefully.

"5" indicates the condition "Good." The object is exhibitable and requires only maintenance to stay in the present condition.

With this simple priority ranking you can generate reports of your collection's conservation needs.

Software

At this point you are in a better position than you were to evaluate the proposal of some vendor concerning software.

A computer needs a program to tell it what to do. Indeed, it may need several programs to operate. These programs, to a greater or lesser extent, control what you do with your registration system. Programs are called "software." When you wanted to file something with paper records you bought a file cabinet and some folders. You could pretty much dictate how you were going to use these devices, and the technology was easily understood by almost anyone. The operation of computers is not readily apparent to anyone without some study, and software choices are bewildering in their number and complexity.

You should select the software before you select the hardware. The kind of software we will probably be looking at is so-called application software. An application program is the one you use to perform certain structured tasks on the computer such as word processing, spreadsheets, desktop publishing, and, of course, data management.

The kind of application software that you will probably use for registration is some form of a data management program. These programs will have the ability to create, edit, index, and sort data, and then display the results on the screen or paper. They will have a report-writing utility built in. They will usually have mail-merge ability that allows you to create specialized documents from the data in your collection file with a word processing program. This will be part of the ability to import or export the data to or from other programs or applications. As part of the package, the application program may even have a word processing or a spreadsheet utility.

The best known type of data management program is a "relational database" program.[4] This kind of program relates each piece of data to every other piece. Not all data managers are relational databases, but that does not mean the ones that are not are not as useful. In fact, you probably will not be able to tell one from the other in operation, and the simpler programs may fit the needs of a small historical museum best. All data managers can be programmed to do specific tasks. It is how this programming is done that is important. You will have to analyze the capabilities of the program, particularly the ease of use and, very important, the speed with which it operates.

There are many consultants or companies that take other company's software and adapt it to specific situations. They are called third-party vendors, or resellers, or just vendors, but also value-added dealers (VAD) or value-added retailers (VAR). Almost all your museum-specific computer application programs will come from third-party vendors of one kind or another. There are two choices for you.

- The most easily available is a fully developed collections management application program marketed as a package to the museum field at large. These programs are usually adaptations of existing application programs, but some are written from scratch in one of the available computer languages. I am going to call these "third-party programs." The third-party programs are widely advertised in the professional museum journals, and demonstrated at professional meetings. The opinion of most of the museum people I talk to is that most of these programs are adequate and the simpler the program is, the better.
- The other is a program written specifically for you by a third party. These programs are often adaptations of off-the-shelf application programs, but occasionally they are written from scratch in one of the computer languages. I am going to call these "proprietary programs." These proprietary programs are reinventing the wheel, developing a program that has been done many times before, but can give you a program specifically tailored to your needs.

In dealing with vendors keep in mind this consideration: you are not buying a program; you are buying a registration system! The vendor will be talking about the "program" and you will be talking about the "system." Make sure you are both talking about the same thing!

There are a bewildering number of possibilities and it is difficult enough for an expert to pick the right one, let alone a novice. You will be better able to make a choice if you look at these considerations:

- What do you want the program to do? Is it to be a complete registration system performing all the functions of your old manual registration system? Or is it be an electronic catalogue? If you have made your needs assessment you will be better able to assess this choice.
- Does the vendor have a client list? He or she should. Get the names of nearby museums as much like yours as possible where this software is

installed. *Go and look* at the system in operation. There is nothing like an opinion from a user, or several users, to find out how the program really works. If the vendor has never done a museum program, he or she should be able to supply a list of clients with similar needs as yours.

- Almost all the third-party programs have several screens. A screen is a specific view of a number of the fields in your data bank. You flip from screen to screen looking for specific arrangements of data. Can you easily get to the screen you want or do you have to flip from screen to screen to screen every time you want to look at something? Instead of having the vendor demonstrate to you, sit down at the machine and try it yourself! To be useful, these screens require a lot of data entry. Do you need all this information? Can you enter all of it and keep it updated?

- The manuals that come with the various programs are very important. Many programs no longer supply paper manuals and "help screens" are contained inside the program. When this is done, check to see if the information is actually useful or just some helpful hint. Does the vendor supply you with an electronic or paper manual for his or her adaptations and can you read and understand it? There will undoubtedly be an electronic or paper manual for the data management program that has been adapted for museum-specific use.

- Your data is worthless unless it can be read by a program so the ability of more than one company's program to read your data is a survival characteristic. In looking at the program that your system is based upon, you are going to have to assess the "portability" of the data that is generated by this program. That is the ability to transfer the data to other programs and other computers. The primary reason for this is that programs do not last forever, vendors go out of business, hardware changes, and better programs come along. The other reason is that you may want to use the data in other programs to create useful documents or perform some other function. If you can't make this assessment, then try to get advice from an expert. You have to assume that most widely vended application software programs are portable, but this is not always true. If in doubt, make the vendor show you that the software is!

- You need copies of the disks containing the various programs that actually operate the registration system. Without these disks you cannot make any changes to your program, and perhaps are not able to transport it. Normally, the vendor will give you a package consisting of the program(s), manuals, and anything else that is needed to make it work. But some vendors do not use this method and you must make sure that you have the "source" programs, or the basic applications, that will interact with your computer, or with others. Otherwise, you may not be able to alter, upgrade, or transport your program without the vendor—who may not be available, or with whom you may not wish to do business.

- Can the vendor adapt the package specifically for your museum or must you take it as sold? If the vendor can adapt it, is there a fee for this? If it is as sold, is this what you want?
- Is the program written for your type of museum? Many programs are written for other kinds of museums and then adapted to history museums. A test of usefulness is whether they have a field for classification. If you have done your needs assessment well, then you will be able to make a judgment about the usefulness of the program.
- Does the vendor give on-site training? How much training? Is there a fee for this?
- Does the vendor support the program either over the telephone or online? Is there a charge for this? Check with the people on the vendor's client list on how well he or she does.
- In the case of proprietary programs the program produced should be a "work for hire." That is, the copyright is the museum's property. You should not be restricted in how you can adapt or use the program or which vendor you can use to update it. The original vendor may not be around when needed. Moreover, you do not want to pay a vendor the start-up costs to develop a program that he or she will market widely. On the other hand, the vendor may not want to create a program for you that you will sell or give away far and wide with no benefit to the vendor. You will have to reach an agreement with the vendor on this. I would warn you away from any deal where only the original vendor may update the program.

Do It Yourself

You have another choice. If you are familiar with computers you may be able to adapt an application yourself. You become your own third-party vendor. This may prove to be an excellent way for a small museum that can define its goals and keep things simple. This is also a procedure that the museum has to approach very cautiously. I know two cases where someone worked on one of these adaptations for a long period of time, in both cases for several years, and never produced a useful program.[5]

Any program produced should be in some readily available application program; it should be updatable; and it should be exportable to other programs.

The museum should have an agreement with the staff member doing this on the goals of the program, a timetable, and a measurement of success. Documentation (a user manual) should be part of the package. I would not get into this unless

- The staff member is already familiar with programming or adapting applications. It is not a good idea for someone to learn to program on your time, and make all their mistakes in your museum.
- There is some mutually agreed-upon measure of the success of the program. A simple measurement would be that the program would answer the needs discovered in your needs assessment, be usable by any staff member, be able to do sophisticated searches (find all the bow back Windsor chairs made in Hero County before 1800), be able to produce a certain number and type of reports, have a user manual, and have a data dictionary.
- The program can be finished in a specific time frame—usually no longer than a third-party vendor would take to develop the same program.

I adapted an application program at the Old Barracks Museum.[6] I spent three months working with the old records and collection in developing an idea of our needs before I even bought the application program. This advance work would have been needed for any type of program selected. I had the museum's program created and up and running in about four hours, but then I had designed the program to use only one screen. I updated it a little after that as I found things had been forgotten or were never used. I wrote a thirty-page user manual with data standards for the system. I must say that it would have been a lot cheaper to buy one of the museum-specific programs, but the museum did not have the funds, but they did have my salary. Of course, the Old Barracks had a program that fitted their specific needs. I understand it has since been transported to another application program and a different computer, so it has passed that test as well.

Something to Think About

A third-party program will have been tried and tested for applicability in many museums and should be up and running within a few minutes of being installed, but will be designed to fit the needs of a wide range of museums. The proprietary program may suit your needs best, match unusual hardware requirements, and will include things that no other program has, but will take a lot more money, time, and work. The small museum may find that it can keep costs down and usefulness up by creating its own program.

How to Make a Choice

The mass-marketed third-party museum software has a lot to offer small museums. You are in a much better position to evaluate it than any other program, the vendor will have a track record, you can see it in operation in other museums, and the start-up time is minimal. On the other hand, if the museum has needs that are specific to the museum, has unusual hardware requirements, has to make complicated searches, or has to produce sophisticated documents, then proprietary software designed specifically for you may be the choice. Finally, if you can enforce rigid standards, and the museum has a staff member familiar with data management systems, you may be able to write your own program.

Hardware

I have not discussed hardware very much. When you have made all the choices for your software you will find the choice of hardware is relatively simple. You probably cannot have too fast a machine, too much mass storage (hard drive space), or too much RAM memory, but the practical consideration of cost will govern that to some extent. It is a good idea to buy at least twice as much mass storage space as you will ever need, if not more. Three or four times would not be too much.

In dealing with PCs, I would recommend only buying hardware that has a configuration that has a wide popular acceptance—that is, it is made by several manufacturers, and has well-understood industry-wide standards. When you buy a machine with a configuration that only one manufacturer makes, then you are at their mercy, and software choices are more limited.

I am equally reluctant to buy a software program that will run on only one particular manufacturer's computer. This is so-called hardware-specific software. The program for a computer should run on all the machines in its class. Minnies and mainframes may require hardware-specific programs but even then there will be a number of choices in programs. Even with these specialized programs the data should be transportable, though you may have more limited choices.

Free(!) Computers

When a museum "computerizes" it may be offered a free machine by someone. These are usually old but functional devices sitting around in someone's home or business. Computer software becomes obsolete in three years or less and the hardware rarely is up to date that long. The gift computer may be slow and of limited capacity by present standards. The problems with such gifts are many and turning one down may be difficult. As diplomatically as possible, one should try to get a new computer of sufficient size and speed dedicated to collection uses. An argument you might use is that the "free" computer might cost more to update and maintain than a new one.

LANS and WANS

If there are a number of computers in the museum it may pay to set up a local area network (LAN). If they museum has facilities scattered over a region, or is statewide or national, then you may need a wide area network (WAN). These are two different kinds of applications, and may require different hardware and software than each other. These networks are usually very difficult to set up and may require an expert. There may be a savings to offset the cost of these networks as you will have increased ability to communicate, see higher efficiency, may not need as sophisticated a terminal for everyone, and can share software, printers, faxes, and scanners.

Enforcing networkwide discipline requires some sophisticated management techniques. If you install a network on more than two or three machines you had better be prepared to spend some time on administrating the network. Both types of network require extensive security measures, particularly the WAN.

Data Entry and Testing

A program is useless until the data is entered into the data bank. Data entry is a real chore and is the place where many computer projects go wrong. The data in most paper records will not translate easily to a computer record. Until the data conforms to specific standards it will not be very useful. There are several ways to handle the initial capture of information in your file.

- You can develop a "data capture sheet" that has a place for every field in the computer program. This is just a version of the worksheet dis-

---

DATA CAPTURE SHEET
Hero County Historical Society

Name of Object: Accession Number:
Classification: Old Accession Number:

Source: Pair or Set:

Material:

Size:

Place of Origin:

Maker:

Association:

Value:

Date (of manufacture):

Conservation Priority:

Description:

                                             Image No.

Comment:

Figure 17: Data Capture Sheet. This is essentially another form of the worksheet. You should design one of these to fit your own needs. It helps if the data is arranged in the order you enter it. This is the last paper document you generate in the accessioning process. If you do not print out your worksheet you sould archive this form.

cussed earlier. You can update the data as you enter it on the form. Then inexperienced data-entry persons can enter the information into the computer. This may be the best method but it will take a lot longer than other methods before you have entered enough data to be useful, an awful lot longer. See the example of the data capture sheet (figure 17).

- You can update the information as you enter it from the original records. This will require trained people to do the data entry, though they do not necessarily have to be the professional staff. They can be volunteers. I used this system at the Old Barracks Museum, and found that it was efficient and produced usable data almost instantly.

- Or you can enter the data as it is and update it afterwards. Untrained people can do the data entry, but a trained person is going to have to go through each record and correct it. This is a method that a small museum might consider as you get usable data almost from the start. There are "optical character readers" (OCRs) that may be able to read your old data into your new files. If you have a large collection file, an OCR may be worth exploring.

In any case, the professional staff is going to have to check each record. You can get the computer to do some of the updating for you or at least find some of the errors (such as all the objects without measurements).

To avoid data-entry fatigue early in the process I would suggest a simple procedure. I would suggest a very simple record with only three fields, the number and name of the object and its location. Any unskilled data-entry person can do this and you will end up with a complete file of your collection. Then you can go back and round off each record.

Data Dictionary

You will need a "data dictionary." This is a document that sets standards for data. You might be able to tell that "stockings, pair," "stockings, pr," "pair of stockings," and "stockings (a-b)" all mean the same thing, but a computer cannot without very complicated instructions. For most applications you will have to pick one way or another to enter data, and you must establish similar standards for each data field. On the other hand, you can configure fields to accept only certain types of data, or only accept certain words, or to make the field conform to a standard, or automatically adapt the data to your specifications. This ability mitigates, to a limited extent, the need for rigid standards.

Testing Your Data

When you start up a program it is a good idea to enter a few records and test the system. Enter about one hundred records and try it out. You will discover many of the problems of data entry and idiosyncrasies of the program. Later, when you have one thousand or so records, you ought to do this again. A file of the latter size will also give you an idea of how much space the whole file is going to take up on your disk, and give you an accurate estimate of the time required to enter all the museum records.

Many museums find that volunteers can enter data if they have some training. Entering data is the most expensive part of the project and using volunteers can save you a lot of money. Once the volunteers are trained, they are a pool of people who are familiar with your system and can do all sorts of jobs for you.

How Many Objects Do You Have?

An interesting question comes up when you begin to the enter data into a computer: this is, how many objects does the museum have? For things such as a pair of andirons, a pair of stockings, a cup and saucer, a fireplace set, or a chess set, is there one record or several? In a paper catalogue they are often listed as one object or, at least, on one card. There is quite a bit of discussion in the museum field about this question with little resolution. How you treat this depends on the kinds of results you need from the catalogue. If you are just looking for a simple catalogue system then perhaps treating objects en suite with others as a single object will work. Because the computer itself is not able to make judgments on how to look at this kind of quandary, I favor treating each unit of a set as a single record (except pairs of shoes, stockings, and gloves). It gives you a better idea of the size of the collection, you can track condition of each object better, you can make more sophisticated searches, and you can predict the cubic volume of the collection better. That means when you have a chess set you do not have one object but thirty-four: the thirty-two chess pieces, the board, and the box the set comes in.

If you make an individual record for each object in a pair or set you may want to add a field to indicate that this object is part of a pair or set. I have a field for pairs and sets that lists the accession number of the first object in the suite.

Cost

Suppose you have just recatalogued your museum's collection and face retyping two cards on each object in our 10,000-object museum. If it only costs you a dollar to type a card, and you have two cards on each object, then you have $20,000 in catalogue cards alone, plus a 10- or 15-drawer file cabinet. Depending on the nature of the data, you can own a good-sized computer and have all your data entered for about that much money.

Cards are usually typed on existing equipment one at a time by a staff person and the cost does not appear as a separate line item on the books of the museum. You have to buy the computer and its supporting software and do the data entry as line items. That makes the project appear as a huge cost. Averaged over the life of the computer, and the usefulness of the data, a computer system does not cost anywhere near as much as manually creating, maintaining, and updating a card file. This is something you should consider when making the choice between manual or computer records, and when you update your files.

People tend to think of the hardware as the most expensive thing in the registration system, but the most expensive thing is the data. It costs a lot to create and maintain it. As an example, at the Old Barracks, we had less than

$2,000 worth of equipment and software, but about $15,000–$20,000 worth of data.

Updates

It is a lot more complicated to keep the computer file up to date than the old paper records. You will find yourself spending a lot of time updating the records. One of the advantages of the computer is that an active updating process will make the system much more useful as time goes on.

While a good paper system is good for decades, the useful life of your hardware and software is about five years, if that. Think carefully about making a long-term commitment to any hardware or software configuration. You will easily have at least three computer programs that will need to be constantly updated: the adaptation of the application program you are using, the application program itself, and the computer's system program(s). The hardware itself becomes obsolete with amazing rapidity. The museum should budget at least 15 or 20 percent of the total cost of the system each year over the life of the system just for updates. Occasionally you will need more.

Security

Although the security of the records of any system is important, the security of computer files is a serious concern. It is not difficult for a well-meaning person to completely destroy your data bank in a few minutes, and there are people out there who are not well meaning. For this reason access to the computer must be limited to the few people who can be trusted not to compromise your data. Most data managers allow various levels of access to the files through a password system. It is an excellent idea to use passwords and security levels. There are various methods of checking updated files before they are inserted into the database. It is best if only one person be allowed to authorize the changes.

When your computers are on a network, or can be accessed via modem, then you have some real concerns about security. There is probably not a security system in the world that cannot be bypassed by a determined person, but you can keep most people out with "firewall" programs. There is also encryption. Depending on how much access you are going to allow to your records via networks and outside access, I would suggest setting up some sort of block that will restrict outside access to only those records, and those fields, that are public.

There are programs called "viruses." These are programs that ride into your system on the backs of other programs or data and can completely corrupt your system. You should have an up-to-date virus protection program installed.

The programs that operate your registration system are very important. The disks should be "archived," that is, locked up in a secure place along with your backups. A secure place is not only safe from pilferage but also of ideal climate, fireproof, and free of electromagnetic interference.

Backups

You never faced losing your whole registration system in a fraction of a second until you got a computer. There is no excuse for losing your data. You need to back up your files regularly on disks or tape. Two or three times a day is not too often. There is a kind of backup where the system verifies that it is a correct and complete copy. You should make one of those at the end of the day. It is a good idea to keep two or three days' worth of backups in reserve. In case of discovering badly corrupted data, you can then go back before the problem started, and rescue your files.

You should have at least three backups at the end of the day. One of the backups should be kept in a fireproof place in the museum, perhaps a safe if you have one, and one off-site. You can buy programs that will back up your files or provide off-site storage, and most application programs contain some sort of backup utility. Even a small collection develops a huge computer file and you will probably need one of those large-capacity removable disks.

It is a good idea to make a paper backup periodically. This is a difficult question to decide and will be governed by the size of your collection and needs. It might take four, six, or more hours to print 2,500 records. A printing of only 10,000 records may take 15 or 20 hours and be a stack of paper several feet high. You may not want to do this very often. There are computer service houses that will do this for you at a relatively modest cost if they have compatible software. Electronic backups can substitute for paper but keep in mind electronic records do not last without some updating on your part.

Remember something about paper records! They tend to last. Computer programs deteriorate over time and need constant care. Your application program may get so old it is useless (although CDs apparently will outlast paper, but your hardware and applications must be able to read them). Without a proper application program you cannot read your files. Printed on archive-quality paper a computer record will survive for a very long time. In fire-resistant cabinets, paper will survive almost any fire and a wetting, something a computer cannot.

Since a computer file is in a constant state of update you will want to keep a picture of your collection at a certain period of time. It is a good idea to archive a backup every so often. Once a year is usually enough, but also just before you make a major update, and other needs may require other solutions.

A Computer Has Other Uses than Registration

To a small museum the computer offers many other advantages in addition to its usefulness in the registration system. Even a very small computer can give you a sophisticated word processing program (often with the ability to set type for newsletters, other publications, and labels), an ability to handle membership lists, an ability to schedule tours and events, a method of forecasting budgets, an accounting system, a data file for such tasks as fund-raising and address lists, and many other uses. The small museum may need these things long before it needs to place its registration system in some electronic data form.

What Not to Do and When Not to Do It

Don't make a needs analysis. Go down to your local computer store and buy the first data management program you see on its looks. Set up a database without reading the manual. Start entering data from the first record at hand. Do not make a commitment of time to the project. Do not learn anything about computers, and never update your programs or equipment. I can guarantee that you will have some interesting moments. I actually have seen systems where this has been done.

Conclusion

The computer can perform some very sophisticated tasks for you very quickly and efficiently, but knowledge of the computer, software, application, and practices needs constant updating to be effective. If you learned to type when I did (the 1940s), you learned a skill that will last your lifetime. A computer skill lasts about five years at the most without updating. You have to be constantly updating your skills, hardware, and software. A museum has to take a very long view with a computer.

Regardless of whether you use a computer or not, you are still going to have to follow a set of practices similar to the ones outlined in this book. A computer offers a solution to many of the complications of a registration system and I expect that most museums will have them before very long if they do not already. Just remember, the computer is a tool just like any other tool and do not get carried away by the technology.

Notes

1. I am going to use the word "computer" for a device that uses and manipulates data in an electronic form. There is no single source for the use of computers in museums that is recent enough to be useful, but there is plenty else written about them. Buck and Gilmore, *New Museum Registration Methods* has a considerable amount on computers scattered through the book. See particularly Suzanne Quigley, "Documentation: Computerized Systems," in Buck and Gilmore, *New Museum Registration Systems*, 17–40.

2. Daniel B Reibel, "Classification Systems and the Size of the Registration Systems," *ALHFAM Proceedings* 27 (2005), 160–161. Delivered as an address before the ALHFAM annual meeting in 2005.

3. See Blackaby, *Nomenclature*: Lanzi et al., *Introduction to Vocabularies*.

4. The term "database" is thrown around a lot but refers only to a particular type of data storage. A more generic term is "data bank."

5. For a good example, see Paul E. Rivard and Steven Miller, "Cataloging Collections—Erratic Starts and Eventual Success: A Case Study," in Fahy, *Collections Management*, 211–214.

6 . The Old Barracks Museum is an eighteenth-century barracks in Trenton, New Jersey, administered by the Old Barracks Association.

Conclusion: The Final Word

All of this may seem overwhelming, but if you tackle each task as it comes up you will find the job goes smoothly enough. It takes a real commitment to register the whole collection, but once done the maintenance of the system is fairly simple. If you plan carefully, commit enough time and resources to the task, and stick to it until done you will find the rewards are worth the effort.

APPENDIX A

~

Forms

Forms are necessary as they make sure that

- All the information is captured in an order useful to the museum.
- Museum policy is carried out.
- There is an accounting trail so that all parties can account for their actions.

The trick is to have as few forms as possible.

With the computer being so ubiquitous, the nature of forms has changed. If the registration system is computerized the need for most forms disappears, and the ones used can be generated by the computer. In many cases, even such sacred things as ledgers and registers are kept in electronic form. Many of the forms now exist only as a particular screen in the registration program. Even in a manual system, the forms, or their formats, are often generated in-house by a computer.

At one time I would have printed the actual forms as a guide for the (human) printer. Forms, if they are used at all, are now mainly produced in-house on the (computer) printer.

Many of the examples of how the forms are used appear in the text. The forms in this appendix are listed roughly in the order they appear in the book. They are numbered sequentially from A-1 (for form 1 in appendix A) to A-14. This citation is used when the forms are referred to in the text.

For more on forms see the following books: Buck and Gilmore, *New Museum Registration Methods*, *passim*; Malaro, *Primer*, *passim*, for several succinct forms; and to please lawyers Phelan, *Museum Law*, *passim*, for many detailed forms. There is a large assemblage of forms in John M. A. Thompson et al., eds, *Manual of Curatorship*, especially Sheila M. Stone, "Documenting Collections," 127–135, and many forms following British practice and also Light, 1986. It is out of print but Kenneth D. Perry, *The Museums Form Book*, 3rd ed. (Austin: Texas Association of Museums and Mountain-Plains Museums Association, 2000) has many forms actually used by museums.

List of Forms Found in Appendix A

A-1. Certificate of Gift Form
A-2. Printed Acknowledgment of Gift
A-3. Justification for Accession Form
A-4. Worksheet
A-5. Accessions Register
A-6. Example of Typed Accession Ledger Page
A-7. Catalogue Cards
A-8. Inventory Form
A-9. Loan Form for Loans from the Museum
A-10. Loan Form for Loans to the Museum
A-11. Deposit Loan Forms
A-12. Condition Report
A-13. Loan Register

List of Forms Found in Text

A-1 Certificate of Gift Form

The format needs to agree with the laws of your state so it needs to be looked at by a lawyer. The form should contain these provisions:

1. The donor owns the object(s) and has the right to dispose of it.
2. The donor is freely giving them to the museum.
3. The donor is surrendering all rights to the objects including copyright and trademark (if he or she owns them).
4. The donor understands that the museum
   - Will display the object at its discretion
   - May not keep collections together
   - Reserves the right to dispose of (deaccession) the object at its own discretion
5. There is a place for a signature from a responsible party from the museum.
6. There is a place for a signature from the donor(s).
7. There is a place for witnesses' signatures, if required.
8. The date the form was signed.

[If the copyright or trademark is not passed to the museum, or is restricted in any way, this should be noted.]

It should be clear that the gift is to the museum. The use of this form implies that you are taking the object into your collection. It is the first step in accessioning the object(s). You should use another kind of form if you are taking the object in for purposes other than inclusion in your collection.

One should consult Malaro, *Primer*, 52*ff*, and Phelan, *Museum Law*, 273*ff*, before developing any gift agreement form. This form, and loan documents, are things best approved by the museum's attorney.

A-2 Printed Acknowledgment of Gift

The Board of Trustees
of the
Hero County Historical Society
gratefully acknowledge
your gift to the collection of the Museum

[a short listing of the donation might go here]

Sincerely,
[signed]
President

This form should be printed on high-quality card stock with a matching envelope. For some reason or another, it looks better when hand addressed with a postage stamp, rather than typed and metered.

A letter is even better. There is an example of one in chapter 2 on acquisitions. Some museums use both a letter and a form.

A-3 Justification for Accession Form

This form is handy as it gives collection committees some real criteria for accepting or rejecting accessions. It makes staffs justify why they want to add
the object to the collection. Later on, it will serve as an answer to why the
museum thought the object important enough to accession, should the question ever come up. These are the questions that should be answered on the
form. These criteria were developed by Bruce Bazalon in the 1980s, then registrar of the Pennsylvania Historical and Museum Commission.

- Does the object have a provenance, coherent history, or identification
  linking it to the museum's purpose?
- Does the object duplicate another object in the museum's collection?
- What is the condition of the object?
- Does it, or will it, need conservation?
- What will this cost?
- Can the museum take care of the object?
- If the museum does not accept it, what will happen to it?
  - If it is sold on the open market will its history be lost?
  - Will it be destroyed?
- If the museum is buying the object, does its value reflect market cost?

A-4 Worksheet

If neatly printed on good paper, this form will do as an accession sheet.

WORKSHEET

Hero County Historical Society

Name of Object: Accession Number:
Old Number (if there is one):
Classification (if using *Nomenclature*):
Source: Address:
Method of Acquisition: Date:
Special Terms of Acquisition:
Value:
Location:
Physical Condition:
Description:

Part of a Pair or Set?   Material:
Place of Manufacture:
Maker/Artist/Designer/Manufacturer/Distributor: (This can be combined with the User field)

User(s):   Date:
Place of Use:
Association with Person, Place, Event, or Social, Ethnic, etc., Group:

Marking, Inscriptions:

Measurements:
Provenance:
Compiler:
Comments:

The fields in this worksheet are an adaptation of fields suggested by the Common Agenda Data Bases Task Force (1989). If you are using a computer database, some of these fields can be included in the description. The fields should be arranged in the order they are to be entered or typed on the card or in the computer.

It goes without saying that if you do not intend to track the information in a field, then do not include it on your form, or capture it in your computer data bank. There are 25 fields on this form, making a potential of a total of 250,000 entries for a museum with 10,000 objects. Make sure you can handle that much data before you incorporate every field on this form. Remember, I suggest less than 20 fields for a computer data bank.

A-5 Accessions Register

This register is for a manual system. It is used *before* the object is accessioned. Its main purpose is to keep track of numbers. It gives you a quick view of the whole collection. The example is from a three-number system. If the single-number or two-number systems are used, you will need to list every object.

Computer systems will be able to generate this ledger, if needed, *after* the objects are accessioned. An example of a computer-generated register is in the text.

Acc. No.	Objects	Source	Date
008.1	Set of china, ca. 1770–1800, 42 pcs.	Mary Jones (Mrs. Charles)	2/13/08
008.2	Plow plane, ca. 1880	William Carpenter	3/2/08
008.3	Tuba	Johannes S. Bach	3/21/08
etc.			

A log would be very similar to this, but kept in a stenographer's notebook. There is an example in the text.

A-6 Example of Typed Accession Ledger Page

February 19, 2008
Gift of: Mr. & Mrs. Loyal Descendent
         (in the name of Noble Ancestor)
         123 Beesom Street
         Hero, Franklin 15555

75.11.1 <u>Machine, broom making</u>: Consists of a rotating clamp held by a ratchet; clamp is hollow to hold broom handles; in back is device to hold wire, consisting of crank-turned square bar on which slides a wooden spool; whole meant to fit on bench; base vaguely L-shaped; whole painted black; 37½ × 27¼ × 10½ overall.

75.11.2 <u>Clamp, broom</u>: Consists of two iron jaws worked by a lever; jaws can be raised and lowered by a ratchet and crank mechanism on left; one guide (right rear) broken; whole stands of two pieces of wood to working height; molded on lip of jaws is "Pat'd Sep. 10, 1876"; painted black; 43¾ × 14 × 30 (less handle) over all; 34" to top of handle with jaws closed.

75.11.3 <u>Cutter, broom</u>: Consists of a tapered wooden trough; at small end is cutter of cast iron which pivots on one end and is worked by handle; a series of holes is drilled in cutter making legend, "W & D York Pa."; meant to sit on legs (missing); painted black; 44 1.4 × 28 1.2 × 12½ overall with handle down.

Note: The above items belonged to Mr. Descendant's great-uncle, William Jones (early 20th century), a broom maker, who built house at 123 Beesom Street in 1920.

acc/DBR/mc

This form can be generated from a computer data bank, if needed.

A-7 Catalogue Cards

Examples of catalogue cards are illustrated in chapter 6. Keep in mind that catalogue cards are not the complete accession record, but just the information you immediately need. If necessary, the card should lead you to the proper record.

At a minimum, the catalogue card should have the name of the object and the accession number. The examples give you about the maximum and minimum information needed on a catalogue cards.

Notice that the name of the museum appears on the bottom of the card. The information you want is at the top. The name identifies the origin of the card.

Example of a main entry card:

Object: Plate, Dinner	**Acc. No.**: 952.2.1
Class: 04 Food Service	
Source: Ivy Propan	
Material: Pottery	**Size**: 11.375 dia. × .875
Maker: Clews	**Place**: England
Date: ca. 1830	**Association**: Lafayette

Description:
Flat bowl with curving sides; marly curves up; lip faintly scalloped; foot ring; underglaze blue transfer of landing of Lafayette over white ground; on bottom is stamp between two circles, "Clews Warranted safe [illegible]"; and, in underglaze blue, "The Landing of Lafayette at Castle Garden New York 16th August 1824."

Hero County Historical Museum

In this example the name of the museum is placed at the bottom of the card and more useful data on top.

A-8 Inventory Form

Acc. Number	Object	Location	Comment

You use something like this when there are no records. If you use this form with good records you will have to do a lot of flipping through records as the objects will be arranged in the order you found them. There are better ways to do this than using this format. Moving cards from one drawer to another is one. If you have a computer, you can generate a list and check off items as found.

A-9 Loan Form for Loans from the Museum

The loan form should contain this information:

- What is actually being borrowed
- The purpose of the loan
- How the object is to be cared for if particular provisions are required
- Method of transportation and who is responsible for arrangement and payment, with a statement that the museum is only responsible for payment for shipment to the named address
- The conditions under which the object will be displayed
- The exact location at which the object will be
- The exact dates of the loan, wall to wall
- The fair market value of each object
- The type and nature of the insurance and who is responsible for it
- A clause detailing conditions if the loan is terminated early
- A statement about how the conditions of the loan are to be amended
- A statement that the total agreement is contained in the form and attachments, and no other conditions apply
- Special conditions
- Conditions for protecting intellectual rights and controlling the use of photography
- The name and signature of the responsible parties
- Date of signatures

An example of typical conditions for a loan follows.

Conditions Concerning Loans from the Hero Count Historical Society

The Hero County Historical Society lends items from its collection only to museums, historical societies, libraries, other educational organizations, and approved conservators that, according to the Society, can comply with the conditions stated below.

The conditions, as stated on this form, and any attachments, represent the total agreement between the Hero County Historical Society (hereafter "The Society"), and the individual, institution, or agency borrowing the object(s) (hereafter "The Borrower"). No other terms are binding on The Society. The objects are loaned for the purposes and the times stated on this form. This form is not valid unless signed by a qualified representative of The Society.

The Borrower is required to have an all-risk fine arts insurance policy from an insurance company licensed to do business in the State of Franklin on all objects included on this form, at the value stated, with The Society listed as an additional insured. The Borrower will furnish The Society with a certificate of insurance with a 120-day cancellation clause.

Objects are to be displayed at the place designated and in the manner approved by The Society. All objects listed on this form are in the condition stated. Object(s) loaned will not be exposed to extremes of temperature, strong light, humidity, noxious fumes, etc., and are to be protected from handling by visitors. The Borrower is required to promptly report any damages to the object(s) in this agreement to The Society. The Borrower will not clean, restore, or conserve the object(s) covered by this agreement unless written approval is given by The Society.

The Borrower may take photographs of the object(s) for record purposes. A single photograph may be taken of each object for a one-time publication in a catalogue or similar use approved by The Society. The Society is to receive a copy of all photographs taken of the object(s). No other photography or any other form of reproduction or publication is allowed without the written permission of The Society.

The objects will be shipped via the agent and method stated on this form. Packing, crating, and shipping are the responsibility of The Borrower under conditions agreed to by both parties.

The Borrower will credit The Society in all labels, publicity, publications, and public releases of information unless otherwise directed.

The Borrower agrees to keep The Society informed in writing of all changes in address and ownership that affect this agreement. The agreement, and the object(s) listed may not be transferred to a third party without the expressed written agreement of The Society. In the event of a change in address and ownership of The Borrower it is The Borrower's obligation to notify the lender within five (5) working days.

This agreement may be terminated by either party thirty (30) days after a written notice has been delivered to the other party. A registered letter is considered adequate notice. The party terminating the agreement is responsible for the cost of shipping. The Society agrees to pay only the cost of shipping that does not exceed shipping to the original address.

This agreement may only be amended by written approval of both parties and such amendments must be attached to this agreement.

A-10 Loan Form for Loans to the Museum

The criteria for loans to the museum are pretty much the same as loans from, only this time the lender makes conditions the museum must follow. As a practical matter, this form will be used mainly with private lenders. Other museums will insist that you use their form.

- What is actually being borrowed
- Description
- Condition
- The purpose of the loan
- How the object is to be cared for if particular provisions are required
- Method of transportation and who is responsible for arrangement and payment, with a statement that, upon return of the object, the museum is only responsible for payment for shipment to the named address
- The conditions under which the object will be displayed
- The exact location at which the object will be
- The exact dates of the loan, wall to wall
- The fair market value of each object
- The type and nature of the insurance and who is responsible for it
- The name and signature of the responsible parties
- A clause detailing conditions if loan is terminated early
- A statement about how the conditions of the loan are to be amended
- A statement that the total agreement is contained in the form and attachments, and no other conditions apply
- Special condition
- Conditions for protecting intellectual rights and controlling the use of photography
- A place for signatures of responsible parties
- Date of signatures

An example of typical conditions for a loan follows.

Conditions Governing Loans to the
Hero County Historical Society

The conditions, as stated on this form, and any attachments, represent the total agreement between the Hero County Historical Society (hereafter "The Society"), and the individual, institution, or agency lending the object(s) (hereafter "The Lender"). No other terms are binding on The Society, The objects are loaned for the purposes and the times stated on this form. This form is not valid unless signed by a qualified representative of The Society.

The Society will treat the object(s) as if they were part of The Society's collection. The condition of the object is as stated on this form or attachments.

The Society agrees to compensate The Lender, through The Society's insurance company, for any loss or damage to the object(s) up to the value listed on this form. If The Lender elects to maintain his/her own insurance, he/she must furnish The Society with a certificate of insurance for the value listed with a 120-day cancellation clause from an insurance company licensed to do business in the state of Franklin with The Society named as an additional insured.

The term of the loan is as stated. The loan may be terminated by either party thirty (30) days after written notice to terminate is delivered to the other party. A registered letter is sufficient notice of termination. The party canceling the loan will pay for packing and return shipment, but in no case will The Society pay more than the cost of shipment to the address named on this form.

The Society reserves the right to photograph the object for record purposes. Such photograph will be restricted to the files of The Society. A copy of such photographs will be given to The Lender. All other conditions concerning photography and publication appear on the face of this agreement or in attachments.

The Society will credit The Lender in all labels, publicity, and publications unless otherwise directed.

The Lender agrees to keep The Society informed in writing of all changes in address and ownership. In the event of a change in address and ownership The Society agrees to pay only the cost of shipping that does not exceed shipping to the original address.

If The Lender cannot, or will not, receive his/her objects back within ninety (90) days after the termination of this agreement, The Society reserves the right to exercise a lower standard of care, and/or charge a storage fee, and/or to take title to the object(s) in a manner described by law. A registered letter to The Lender's last known address is sufficient notice of The Society's intention to return the object(s) in this agreement.

This agreement may only be amended by written approval of both parties.

A-11 Deposit Loan Forms

Deposit loans are very much like any other loan to the museum except

- The loan is for a maximum of thirty days.
- The museum does not agree to pay for any damage of loss except in the case of gross negligence.
- Pickup and delivery is usually the responsibility of the lender.

The clause governing the conditions of the loan might read like this:

It is understood that the object(s) listed on this form are left at the museum for temporary deposit and the museum accepts no responsibility for them other than due care. The lender is responsible for pickup and delivery. The condition is as stated on this form.

A-12 Condition Report

Most museums won't have a conservator on staff who can give technical answers to one of these reports, so the form has to be tailored for the museum staff. The form should have slots that require a written answer, not a checkmark, to all conditions. You need a form for each object. A form should require specific answers for these things:

- Catalogue description of the object.
- Whether this form is just a routine report of condition or reporting damage.
- If damage is reported, the nature of it, and where, when, and how and who first noted it.
- Any work required.
- Estimated costs.
- Accession number and name of object.
- Overall condition of object.
- The condition of the finish.
- The condition of the structure.
- The condition of the materials making up the object.
- The condition of parts, and if there are parts missing.
- If there is a mechanism, does it work? Is it complete?
- How clean is the object?
- Is there any inherent vice?
- A listing of old repairs.
- Any recommendations.
- The date the form was completed.
- Who made out the form?

A-13 Loan Register

Loan registers are like other registers—they only need to contain enough information to help you find the right record. A typical loan register might look like this:

Loan No.	Object	Lender	Date In	Date Out

There is a comment on numbering loans in chapter 3.

~

A Registration Manual for a Volunteer-Run Museum

Hero County Historical Museum

The purpose of this manual is to create a policy and procedure to insure that the Hero County Historical Society will have a registration system that will develop a collection, that will serve the purposes of the Museum, that will register the collection properly, that will preserve all the information on each object, and that will be in conformance with the highest standards of the museum profession.

Statement of Purpose or Mission Statement

The statement of purpose (or the mission) of the Hero County Historical Society states:

[The statement of purpose of the historical agency should appear here.]

[The organization may have a charter, a constitution, and bylaws. The portions affecting collections should appear here.]

[If there is a collection management policy statement separate from the statement of purpose, that should appear here. A sample collections management policy statement appears below.]

To direct these aims, the Board of Trustees has adopted the following collection management policy.
[*Example*]

Collection Management Policy

The Hero County Historical Society will collect only those items related to the purposes of the Museum, for which it has an ultimate use, and that the Museum can properly store, preserve, and protect. There will be a Collections Committee with the responsibility for developing and implementing a set of registration and collections care practices for the Museum. The manual developing this will be the collections policy of the Corporation, and will contain the necessary procedures. At the Annual Meeting the Collections Committee will report for the Board's approval on the state of the collection and on all new accessions, loans, and deaccessions for the year. In pursuance of these policies the Collections Committee submits this manual to the Board of Trustees.

> Respectfully submitted,
> Collections Committee
> Adopted by the Board of Trustees on _____.

Collections Committee

There will be a Collections Committee composed of at least four members. The Chairperson of this Committee must be a member of the Board, but any member of the Corporation is eligible to serve on the Committee. The Committee will have the general supervision of the collection. The Collections Committee is a standing committee of the Hero County Historical Society.

Curator or Registrar

The Collections Committee, with the approval of the Board, may appoint a Curator and/or a Registrar, who shall be members of the Committee. The Curator will be responsible for the care of the collection, and the Registrar will be responsible for the care of the records of the collection. These members of the Committee will serve an indefinite term at the pleasure of the Board.

Registration File Cabinet

The Committee will acquire a good four-drawer legal-sized fireproof file cabinet with a lock. The cabinet should withstand at least 1,700 degrees Fahrenheit for one-half hour and should have an Underwriters seal. The Committee will place all existing records in that file. It will become the "Registration File Cabinet." The cabinet should be kept locked at all times. The Chairman of the Collections Committee will have a key or the combination, and there will be a copy of the key or combination in the Corporation's safe-deposit box. On the recommendation of the Committee, the Board may assign keys or combinations to other members of the Committee.

Registration and Accession File
The Committee will create an Accession File for each year. All the information on each accession in the year will be in this file. The Committee will create other files on the registration system as needed. These files will be kept in the Registration File Cabinet.

Acquisition
When a donor offers to donate to the Museum an item or items, the Committee will have him or her sign a Gift Agreement Form. No object may be taken into the Museum unless this form is signed. There shall be three (3) copies of this form: one for the donor, one for the Corporation, and one (the original) for the Committee. All donors should be informed that items are accepted subject to the approval of the Board. The original form should be filed in the Accession File.

In the instance of a purchase, the bill of sale and all other documents will be placed in an Accession File. Before the Treasurer disposes of any canceled check, those related to collections should be placed in the proper Accession File.

No member of the Board of Trustees, or of the Museum Committee, may evaluate an object offered for gift. Where such evaluations are requested, the Society will confine itself to cooperating with a qualified appraiser, who is retained by the donor.

Accession Register
The Committee will acquire a well-bound record book for the Museum's use as a register. The first one hundred pages should be left blank to record the existing collection. At the beginning of the next page, the Registrar will write the year this manual is adopted _____ and columns for the accession numbers, types of objects, the sources, and the dates of acquisition. If a computer is used for the registration system, then the register will be part of that system.

The Committee will take the items existing in the collection at the time this manual is adopted and try to correlate them with existing records and list them in the Register in the same fashion as the new accessions, and enter them in the front of the Register. The Committee will be sure to record all accessions in the Register including the address of the source of the accession and the date of acquisition. All entries into the Register will be in indelible ink. The Register is to be kept in the Registration File Cabinet. All measurements will be in the inch/foot system.

Accession Ledger

The Collections Committee will have the Accession Records typed on high-quality archival paper and bound at some convenient interval, say each year. There will be two copies of the Accession Ledger: one will be kept in the Museum library under archive conditions; the other will be the use copy. If the registration system is kept in a computer, the ledger will be part of that system.

Accession Number

The Committee will assign the number one (1) to the first object acquired under the new system, the number two (2) to the second, number three (3) to the third, and so on.

At the beginning of each calendar year, the Committee will start a new page in the Accession Ledger for that year, but the numbers will continue in series.

Only one person will keep the Accession Ledger and assign numbers, and if there is a Registrar it will be that person. No one may use a number unless the number before has been used. The number shall be placed on the object in the manner described in Reibel, *Registration Methods for the Small Museum*. The number shall be placed on all documents associated with each accession and those documents filed in the Accession File.

Accession Record

Each object accessioned will have a Worksheet filled in on it. These are to be kept in the Accession File Cabinet until copied and bound in the Accession Ledger.

Catalogue Card

The information on each Worksheet will be copied onto a catalogue card. These will be filed alphabetically by the title of each object.

Donor File

At the end of each calendar year, the Registrar shall make up a file of donors and other sources. The card file shall contain the donor's or source's name and the accession number associated with each name. Only one card shall be made on a donor.

Acknowledgment of Gifts

Each gift to the collection shall be acknowledged by the Collections Committee, either with a Gift Form, or by letter, thanking the donor for the gift on behalf of the Corporation. A copy of this form or letter, with the accession number(s) on it, shall be placed in the Accession File. All gifts displayed in the Museum must bear the name(s) of the donor(s) in this fashion, "Gift of XYZ." From time to time, the Committee shall supply the Publications Committee with a list of donors for publication in the Newsletter.

Deaccessioning

It is the policy of the Corporation to deaccession as few items from the collection as possible. From time to time, the Collections Committee may wish to remove items from the collection for the following reasons: the item is not germane to the collection; it duplicates a better example; it is a fake or not as represented; its condition threatens itself or the rest of the collection; or the Museum cannot take care of the object properly. On the Committee's recommendation, the Board, with two-thirds of the total membership in attendance approving, may declare an item deaccessioned. The deaccessioned item should be sold at public auction, traded or donated to another educational agency, or destroyed. No deaccession item may be conveyed in any manner to a member of the Board, a member of the Collections Committee, or to anyone holding a post of trust or honor in the Corporation. Funds acquired from deaccessioning must be used to purchase other objects for the collection, or to conserve items in the collection.

Loans

Loans to the Museum shall only be for the purpose of enhancing the Museum's exhibits. The lending party will sign the properly executed loan form. The loan will be insured, using the Museum's carrier. The loan will be approved by the Committee and submitted for approval to the Board of Trustees at their next regular meeting.

Loans from the Museum may only be made for purposes of display in an exhibit which enhances the Corporation's purpose. The borrower will sign a properly executed loan form. The borrower shall furnish proof of insurance or of financial responsibility. Loans from the Museum must be approved in advance by the Board of Trustees.

Objects may not be borrowed or lent for a period of more than one year, but may be renewed from year to year for a total period of three years.

Report to the Board of Trustees

The Collections Committee shall submit a report to the Board of Trustees, at the Annual Meeting, submitting a written report on all new accessions for the year, all outstanding loans, and commenting on the general condition of

the collection, a statement of work achieved, and any other matter it deems necessary.

Copy of the Records

At the end of the calendar year, the Committee shall have the records for the year copied. This shall include all documents, pages in the Accession Ledger, and copies of correspondence. The master copy of this shall be kept in [a safe place away from the Museum]. Another copy shall become the working record for the Museum.

Protection of Intellectual Assets

For the purposes of this policy, the intellectual assets of the Society consist of the images of objects and documents in the collection, the image of the Museum building, the images and content of programs, physical copies of objects in the collection, and dissimilar devices. When permission is made to photograph, copy, or otherwise use this intellectual property, permission is limited to a one-time use for specific purposes. A blanket, long-term, or unlimited use of intellectual property may not be granted under any circumstances.

Ethics

All actions of the Board should be such that it avoids an apparent as well as an actual conflict of interest with any aspect of the Museum operation and its collection. The members of the Board will follow the practices in *Code of Ethics for Museums* (Washington, DC: AAM, 1994).

Amending the Registration Manual

The Collections Committee may suggest amendments to this manual to the Board. Upon approval these amendments will become part of this manual.

* * *

The documents and forms implementing this manual are attached as a reference.

APPENDIX C

~

Example of a Museum Collection Policy for a Museum with Professional Staff

Collections Management Policy and Manual
Hero County Historical Society Museum

This document contains the policy and practices governing the Museum collection of the Hero County Historical Society.

This manual was developed by the Museum Committee consisting of the following members.

XXXXXXXXXXXXXXXXXXXXXXXXXX, Chairperson

XXXXXXXXXXXXXXXXXXXXXXXXXX

XXXXXXXXXXXXXXXXXXXXXXXXXX

XXXXXXXXXXXXXXXXXXXXXXXXX

XXXXXXXXXXXXXXXXXXXXXXXXX

YYYYYYYYYYYYYYYYYYYYYYYYYY, Museum Director, ex officio.

January 26, 20XX

Statement of Purpose

The Statement of Purpose of the Hero County Historical Society as given in the charter which was granted in the Superior Court, County of Hero, the State of Franklin, April 16, 1896, is

[Example]

"The purpose of the Hero County Historical Society shall be to investigate, elucidate, and publish facts on Hero County history; to preserve objects of historical significance; to receive contributions; and to encourage patriotism and public interest in history."

Subsequently, on the adoption of the new constitution of the Society on June 12, 1972, the Board added the provision that this Society be a non-profit organization.

In the bylaws adopted on September 30, 1973, this provision provided for a Museum Committee to operate the Museum.

[Example]

"Article V, Section 7: The Museum Committee shall have the general oversight and direction of the Museum, and shall report to the Board from time to time on the condition of the Museum and the collection. The Museum Committee shall consist of a member of the Board, who shall be chairman, and of at least two other members in good standing of the Society."

Subsequently, upon employing a professional director, the Society adopted this clause to the bylaws on March 4, 1985:

[Example]

"Article XII: The Board may appoint a Museum Director and other staff and set their duties, conditions of work, and compensation. The Museum Director will have the general oversight of the Museum and be responsible for the Museum building, exhibits, program, and collection, and shall have the direction of the staff. The Director shall be an ex officio member of all committees except the Nominating Committee."

Since the original conception of the Society and Museum did not foresee the present nature of our organization, and since the above clauses in our bylaws, as well as other clauses in our charter and constitution, as well as policies and procedures adopted as resolutions over the course of time, do not provide for a modern museum program, this Collections Manual supersedes all provisions in the constitution and bylaws of the respecting Museum and its collection and become the operating document for the Museum collection.

Collection Management Policy

This collections management policy statement is intended to further define the clauses in the constitution and bylaws respecting the Museum collection.

[Example]

It is the policy of the Hero County Historical Society to collect only those items for the Museum that were made and/or used in Hero County; or were associated with a person, place, or event in Hero County; or, to a limited extent, are typical or representative of objects made or used in Hero County; and which are of a historical, cultural, or aesthetic nature, for which the Museum can care for, and which fall in the period of the founding of Hero County.

After complying with the requirements for changes to the constitution and bylaws of the Society, this manual was adopted by the Board of Trustees, Hero County Historical Society, March 26, 20XX.

* * *

Responsibility

The Museum Director is responsible for the Museum and is solely responsible for its collection. The Director will work with the Museum Committee to improve the Museum. He or she, with the approval of the Collections Committee, shall have the authority to accept acquisitions for the Museum collection. He or she shall have the sole authority to make or accept loans. The Director will, from time to time, recommend items from the collection that are to be deaccessioned. The Director will report from time to time to the Board on the condition of the collection. The Museum Committee will act as the liaison in collection matters between the Board and the Director.

Computer and Data Security

The Director is responsible for all the collection records. He or she is solely responsible for assigning access to the records of all types. He or she will assign passwords to other staff as needed. The master password shall be kept in the Museum safe. The Director will archive the original copies of the database application program(s) and such other application programs as may be necessary to extract data. The director shall make a backup of the records on a daily basis. One copy of the backup will be kept with the computer, one copy in the Museum safe, and one off the Museum grounds. A paper backup shall be made and archived every year.

All the registration records and software will be kept in a locked fireproof file cabinet with at least a one-hour fire rating. The cabinet shall be kept closed except when in use. The Museum Director is responsible for the security of this cabinet and shall have a key or the combination. A duplicate key or copy of the combination will be kept by the Secretary in the Society's safe-deposit box.

Before adopting a new data management program, the Director will assure himself or herself that the data managed by this program is transferable to the new program.

Acquisition and Registration

The acquisition of objects should expand and refine the Museum collection and aid in carrying out the Corporation's purpose. The purpose of registration of the Museum objects is to

- preserve any associations with historic events, places, or persons that an object may have;
- promote the preservation of the object itself;
- establish the Society's right of title to the object;
- aid in the interpretation of the object; and
- allow the Society to identify and account for every object in the collection.

Acquisition of an object is after the Director submits copies of a Justification for Accession Form, with a signed Gift Agreement or bill of sale, and any other pertinent document, to the Collection Committee for approval. The Museum will accept no gift in which the Museum's use of the object, or the Museum's right to display or not display the object, is limited in any way, or if the Museum is limited in any way from breaking up collections. However, the Museum may occasionally enter into partial ownership arrangements, life tenures, limited ownerships, or any sharing of title or possession for unique items that will be a significant addition to the collection, but only on advice of attorney, and with the expressed approval of the Board.

Within reasonable limits the Museum may accept restrictions on how the gift will be acknowledged when it is displayed.

[*A section similar to this may be required if there is an existing collection.*]

On adoption of this manual the Director will take immediate steps to see that every object existing in the collection has

1. An accurate Accession Record and description
2. A unique record in the Museum data bank
3. A unique accession number
4. All known documentary information known about the object filed in an accession file and identified by the accession number of the object

[*This section is required in all manuals.*]

All new objects taken into the collection after the adoption of this manual will have the following:

Paper Records

1. A transfer of title document. In the case of gifts this is a valid Gift Agreement. In the case of purchases this is a valid bill of sale. Bequests must have a binding transfer from the estate.
2. A Justification for Accession Form.
3. In the case of gifts, an acknowledgment of gift in the form of a copy of a letter or a form.
4. A unique accession number permanently affixed to the object.
5. An accession file on each accession in a secure file cabinet.
6. Copies of all documents filed in the accession file.

Computer Records

1. A complete record on each object in the Museum data bank. This record will contain enough data in appropriate fields so that the Museum may easily extract the following information:
   a. Management data, or data that relates the object and the records to each other.
   b. Descriptive data, or catalogue information; data about the object that can mainly be acquired by examining the object itself, or from fairly simple research techniques.
   c. Historical data that places the object in a historical context with people, places, or events.
2. The original equipment manufacturers' software for the system software, data management, Museum record keeping, and any other pertinent programs.

Every object will have its own record, including sets and objects en suite with other objects.

The Director will acknowledge all gifts by a personal letter, or may request that an Acknowledgment of Gift be signed by the President.

Accession Number

Each object will be numbered with a unique accession number. The accession number will have a control number, which will be the last two digits of the year of accession (with the exceptions noted below). The second number will be the accession number. In each year the first accession will be assigned the number 1 (one), the second 2 (two), and continuing in strict sequence to the last accession of the year. The third number will be the catalogue number. The catalogue numbers will begin with 1 (one) for the first object in the accession and continue in strict sequence until all the objects in the accession have been numbered. If there is but one object in the accession, it will be given the catalogue number 1 (one).

An example would be the accession number 90.26.3, in which 90 is the year of accession, 26 is the accession number and is the twenty-sixth accession in that year, and 3 is the catalogue number and is the third object in the accession.

In the year 2000, and thereafter, the Museum will add a 0 (zero) in front of the control number, thus 009.92.21.

In the case of the existing collection, the accessions that have known provenance are to be registered with this numbering system. All the objects with an unknown provenance existing in the collection at the time of the adoption of this manual are to be given the accession number 1 (one); in 1990 that would be 90.1.XX, etc.

Nomenclature

The Museum will follow the system developed by Robert Chenhall, *Revised Nomenclature* (Nashville: AASLH, 1988), in naming objects and in classifying the catalogue. The nomenclature shall be confined to terms actually used in the Museum registration system. The computer registration system should be able to produce a lexicon of the terms used by the Museum.

[*The number and types of catalogues will be radically changed if there is a computer. There may not be a catalogue per se, but just the ability to generate certain types of records.*]

Catalogues

The purpose of the Museum catalogue is to give the Museum easy access to the records and collection to aid the Museum staff in accounting. The Museum's registration report should be able to produce the following catalogues, either on-screen or in written reports:

1. All the records by accession number in numerical order.
2. All the objects alphabetically by title.
3. All the objects by source. The report should be able to show the different types of sources (donor, purchase, bequest, etc.).

4. A priority list of conservation needs.
5. All the objects by location.
6. A listing of the value of each object and a total value for the listing.
7. The ability to pull up records by the object's association.
8. Depending on the nature of the Museum's program you may also wish to produce a list of objects on loan *to* the Museum. Under #6 above, the program should already be able to produce a list of objects on loan *from* the museum.
10. The Museum should be able to make "string searches" to extract useful data from the file.

Measurements

All measurements are to be in the inch/foot system. Any computer application program that the Museum acquires must have the ability to convert these to the metric system.

Deaccessioning

The purpose of deaccessioning is to refine the collection so it will help carry out the Society's purpose.

The Museum will only deaccession objects from its collection for the following reasons:

1. Duplication of a better example.
2. The condition of the object threatens itself or the rest of the collection.
3. The object is not germane to the collection.
4. The Museum cannot care for the object properly.
5. The authenticity of the object is questionable.

The Museum will not deaccession objects that have a known history related to our purpose, or that are from living donors, or were accessioned less than twenty-five years previously, unless the object is deteriorated to a point where it threatens itself or the collection or its authenticity is questionable.

Moneys received from deaccessioning may only be used for purchasing new objects for the collection.

Using the Justification for Deaccessioning Form, the Director will recommend that an object be deaccessioned to the Museum Committee. If approved, the Committee will make a similar recommendation to the Board of Trustees. On its approval, the object will be disposed of.

Objects may only be disposed of by a public auction, absolute destruction, or exchange or transfer with another historical agency with a purpose similar to the Society's. No deaccessioned object may be conveyed in any manner to a member of the Board of Trustees, the Museum staff, or anyone holding a post of trust or honor in the Society.

The Museum may exchange or transfer objects in its collection for which it can no longer care or which fit the other criteria of the deaccession process. These transfers or exchanges will be with other museums or educational agencies that can properly care for the object. Any object received in an exchange must fit the Museum's collection policy. Exchanges and transfers must be approved by the Collection Committee and/or Board, as with any other accession or deaccession.

A note that the object has been deaccessioned will be entered on the paper accession record in red ink. Computer records shall be flagged to indicate the object has been deaccessioned.

Loans

The purpose of loans is to enhance the mission of the Society. Loans from the Museum should extend the Society's purpose outside the walls. Loans to the Museum should augment the Society's purpose while increasing the effectiveness of the collection.

The Director has the sole authority to recommend that the Museum lend or borrow objects. He or she will not lend or borrow objects without a properly executed Loan Form.

The Museum may not accept or grant "permanent loans" or loans for a term longer than three years.

Loans to the Museum

The Museum will borrow items for exhibit only using a properly executed Loan Form. The term of the loan will be one year. If the exhibit extends past one year, the loan may be extended for a year, on a year-to-year basis, but for no more than three years in total.

Loans to the Museum will be confined to those objects for which the Museum can care under the same standards as its own collection.

Loans from the Museum

The Museum will lend objects primarily for exhibition in another museum or to a qualified conservator for conservation. Loans from the Museum will only be made on a properly executed Loan Form. Loans may be made to other non-profit educational agencies if the Director is assured that the object will be cared for and displayed in a manner which meets or exceeds Museum standards. Loans will be made only to institutions that have a standard of care equaling or exceeding ours.

The term of a loan from the Museum is one year. For extended loans, the period may be extended for a year on a year-to-year basis but for no longer than three years.

[*The Museum may wish to adopt a clause such as this if the Museum has a number of permanent loans or unknowns in the collection.*]

Permanent Loans and Unknowns
It is the Museum policy to resolve any questions concerning permanent loans and objects with unknown sources as soon as feasible. Immediately after the first inventory of the collection is completed, the Director will prepare a list of permanent loans and objects with unknown sources. The Director will present this list to the Collection Committee with any comments he or she may wish to make. After consideration of this list, the Collection Committee may consult the Museum's attorney and report to the Board any recommendations it may wish to make. The eventual disposition of this class of objects will be made a part of this manual.

Photography of the Collection
The Museum will take a digital image of each object in the collection. These images are intended for identification. They will be catalogued by the accession number of the object. Such number will be clearly visible in each image.

Conservation and Storage
On adoption of this manual, the Director will immediately take steps to prepare a report on the conservation needs of the Museum. The Director will, from time to time, make recommendations to the Board on the conservation of certain objects. The Director will report on the condition of the collection in his or her annual report.

Each record of an object in the Museum registration system will be tagged with a priority number for conservation, where 1 (one) requires the most immediate attention, and 5 (five) requires the least. Objects in the 4 and 5 classification will be considered exhibitable.

Each object will be assigned a permanent location and the object will be said to "live" at that spot. When objects are moved the new location will be tracked.

Inventory

The Museum will inventory its collection each year. The inventory will consist of an examination of each object and the records. The condition of each object shall be noted. Records will be updated as needed. The inventory list for each year will be filed in the accession file.

[*If the Museum insures or places a value on the objects in its collection.*]

Evaluations of the Collection

At the time of accession, the Museum will establish a value for each object in the accession. These values will be used to insure the collection and establish a replacement value for loans from the Museum. These values will be updated, if necessary, during the inventory. These values are confidential and are to be revealed only at the discretion of the Director.

Appraisals

No member of Museum staff, or of the Board of Trustees, or of the Museum Committee, may appraise an object as to its monetary value, or give more than a qualified assessment of identity or age for any object that is not the Museum's property. The Museum will not pay an outside appraiser to establish a value on any object being donated to the Museum. In the case of gifts to the Museum, the Museum, when requested, will confine itself to recommending two or more qualified professional appraisers and cooperating with any appraiser the donor selects.

The director will not evaluate incoming loans but will depend on the owner to supply value. In the case the value is unknown, a suitable appraiser shall be retained.

Properties

The expendable noncollection property of the Museum or Society is not part of this policy or manual. It should be accounted for in a manner recommended by our auditor. Reproductions of authentic objects used in exhibits or demonstrations are properties and should not be accessioned. In the event a property is taken into the collection it shall be accessioned in the regular manner and given the same care as any other item in the collection.

Ethics

All actions of the Board and the Museum staff should be such that they avoid an apparent as well as an actual conflict of interest with any aspect of the

Museum operation and its collection. The members of the Board and the Museum staff will follow the practices in the Ethics Policy adopted by the Board, [Date]. In cases not covered by the Museum's Ethics Policy, the Corporation will follow the American Association of Museums, *Code of Ethics for Museums* (1994).

Protection of Intellectual Assets

For the purposes of this policy, the intellectual assets of the Society consist of the images of objects and documents in the collection, the image of the Museum building, the images and content of programs, and physical copies of objects in the collection. When permission is made to photograph, copy, or otherwise use this intellectual property, permission is limited to a one-time use for specific purposes. A blanket, long-term, or unlimited use of intellectual property may not be granted under any circumstances.

Access

The Museum will grant qualified researchers with legitimate research goals in mind equal access to the collections on a bona fide need-to-know basis. The Director establishes what the qualifications of the researcher and the legitimate goals are. Moreover, the Director may limit access to the object to specified methods of examination and to certain times. The Director may require a written request, stating which objects are to be examined, the method of examination, and the reasons for the examination.

The Museum registration records are not a pubic record but should be considered confidential information. The Director may provide portions of the registration records to qualified researchers, but restrict access to donor, location, and value.

Other Types Of Collections

[*This manual does not cover such items as books, manuscripts, anthropological specimens, etc., which have well-recognized methods of registration. If the Museum has a large enough collection in these other areas, provisions for their care should be incorporated in this manual.*]

Public Document

This policy is a public document. A copy shall be kept in the Museum office and made available to any interested person.

Amendments

This Collections Policy and Manual may be amended by a resolution of the Board of Trustees following provisions in the constitution and bylaws respecting amendments.

* * *

The documents and forms implementing this manual are attached as a reference.

Bibliography

[Note: The American Association of Museums will be referred to as AAM. The American Association for State and Local History will be referred to as AASLH.]

AAM. *Peer Review Manual*. Washington, DC: American Association of Museums, 2005.

AAM Registrars Committee, Professional Practices Subcommittee. "Loan Survey Report." May 1990.

AAM Registrars Committee. *Standard Facility Report*. Professionals Practices Series, AAM Technical Services. Washington, DC: AAM, 1989.

Alten, Helen. "Materials for Labeling Collections." *The Upper Midwest Museums Collections Care Network* 1, no. 6 (Winter 1996), 1–7.

Awerdick, John, and John Kettle III. "Copyright." In Buck and Gilmore, *New Museum Registration Methods*, 289–300.

Baca, Murtha, Patricia Harping, Elisa Lanzi, Linda McRae, and Ann Whiteside. *Cataloging Cultural Objects: A Guide to Describing Cultural Objects and Their Images*. Chicago: American Library Association, 2006.

Blackaby, James B., Chair, Common Data Bases Task Force. "Final Report to the Field, September 1989." *Common Agenda for History Museums*. Nashville: AASLH, 1989.

Blackaby, James C., Chair, Common Agenda Task Force. "Managing Historic Data: Report of the Common Agenda Task Force." *Special Report #3*. Nashville: AASLH, 1989.

Blackaby, James R. *The Revised Nomenclature for Museum Cataloging: A Revised and Expanded Version of Robert G. Chenhall's System for Classifying Man-Made Objects*. Revised and expanded by James R. Blackaby, Patricia Greeno and the Nomenclature Committee. Nashville: The AASLH Press, 1988.

Buck, Rebecca A., and Jean Allman Gilmore. *Collection Conundrums*. Washington, DC: American Association of Museums, 2007.

Buck, Rebecca A., and Jean Allman Gilmore, eds. *The New Museum Registration Methods*. Washington, DC: American Association of Museums, 1998.

Case, Mary, ed., et al. *Registrars on Record: Essays on Museum Collections Management*. Registrars Committee. Washington, DC: AAM, 1988.

Carwell, Clarissa, and Rebecca Buck, "Acquisition and Accessioning." In Buck and Gilmore, *New Museum Registration Methods*, 157–166.

Cowan, Suzanne. "Inventory." In Buck and Gilmore, *New Museum Registration Methods*, 117–119.

DeAngelis, Ildiko. "Old Loans." In Buck and Gilmore, *New Museum Registration Methods*, 281–288.

Duggan, Anthony J., Section Editor. "Collection Management." In Thompson et al., *Manual of Curatorship*, 113–376.

Fahy, Anne, ed. *Collections Management*. Leicester Readers in Museums Studies. New York: Routledge, 1995.

Feldman, Franklin, Stephen E. Weil, and Susan D. Biederman. *Art Law: Rights and Liabilities of Creators and Collectors*. 2 volumes. Boston: Little, Brown & Co., 1986.

Freitag, Sally, and Cherie Summers. "Loans," In Buck and Gilmore, *New Museum Registration Methods*, 177–188.

Guthe, Carl E. *So You Want a Good Museum? A Guide to the Management of Small Museums*. Washington, DC: AAM, 1957.

IMLS. "A Framework of Guidance for Building Good Digital Collections." November 6, 2001.

Keown, C. Timothy, Amanda Murphy, and Jennifer Schansberg. "Ethical and Legal Issues: Complying with NAGPRA." In Buck and Gilmore, *New Museum Registration Methods*, 311–319.

Koelling, Jill Marie, *Digital Imaging: A Practical Approach*. Walnut Creek, CA: AltaMira Press, 2004.

Lanzi, Elisa, et al. *Introduction to Vocabularies: Enhancing Access to Cultural Heritage Information*. Los Angeles: J. Paul Getty Trust, 1998.

Lewis, Geoffrey D. "Collections, Collectors and Museums: A Brief World Survey." In Thompson et al., *Manual of Curatorship*, 7–22.

Lewis, Ralph H. *Manual for Museums*. Washington, DC: National Park Service, 1979.

Light, Richard, et al. *Museum Documentation Systems: Developments and Applications*. London: Butterworths, 1986.

Longstreth-Brown, Kitty. "Documentation: Manual Systems." In Buck and Gilmore, *New Museum Registration Methods*, 1–12.

Malaro, Marie C. *A Legal Primer on Managing Museum Collections*, 2nd edition. Washington, DC: Smithsonian Institution, 1998.

Malaro, Marie C. *Museum Governance: Mission, Ethics, Policy*. Washington, DC: Smithsonian Institution Press, 1994.

Manning, Anita. "Converting Loans to Gifts." *AASLH Technical Leaflet #94.* Nashville: AASLH, 1977.

Morris, Martha. "Deaccessions." In Buck and Gilmore, *New Museum Registration Methods,* 167–176.

Museum Documentation Association. *Practical Museum Documentation,* 2nd edition. Duxford, Cambridgeshire, UK: Museum Documentation Association, 1981.

O'Connel, Brian. *The Board Member's Book: Making a Difference in Voluntary Organizations.* N.p.: The Foundation Center, 1985.

Orlowski, Thomas, J. *Smart Selection and Management of Association Computer Systems.* Washington, DC: American Society of Association Directors, 1995.

Pearsall, Margot P., and Holly B. Uselth. "Registration Records in a History Museum." In Dudley and Wilkinson, *Museum Registration Methods.* Washington DC: AAM, 1979, 245–266.

Perry, Kenneth D. *The Museums Form Book,* 3rd edition. Austin: Texas Association of Museums and Mountain-Plains Museums Association, 2000.

Peterson, Toni, Director. *Art and Architectural Thesaurus.* New York: Oxford University Press, 1994.

Phelan, Marilyn. *Museum Law: A Guide for Officers, Directors and Counsel.* Evanston, IL: Kalos Kapp Press, 1994.

Phelan, Marilyn. *Museums and the Law.* Nashville, TN: AASLH, 1982.

Pointer, Virginia. "Photography." In Buck and Gilmore, *New Museum Registration Methods,* 95–102.

Porter, Daniel R. III. "Current Thoughts on Collections Policy: Producing the Essential Document for Administering Your Collections." *Technical Report 1.* Nashville: AASLH, 1985.

Porter, Daniel R. III. "Developing a Collections Management Manual." *Technical Report 7.* Nashville: AASLH, 1986.

Quigley, Suzanne. "Documentation: Computerized Systems." In Buck and Gilmore, *New Museum Registration Methods,* 17–37.

Racz, Gabor R. "Improving Collection Maintenance through Innovation: Bar-Code Labeling to Track Specimens in the Processing Stream." *Collections* 1, no. 3 (February 2005), 227–241.

Reibel, Daniel B. "Classification Systems and the Size of the Registration Systems." *ALHFAM Proceedings* 27 (2005), 160–161.

Rivard, Paul E., and Stephen Miller. "Cataloging Collections—Erratic Starts and Eventual Success: A Case Study." In Fahy, *Collections Management,* 211–214.

Roberts, D. Andrew. "The Development of Computer-Based Documentation." In Thompson et al., *Manual of Curatorship,* 136–141.

Shapiro, Michael S., Brett L. Miler, Christine Steiner, and Nicholas D. Ward. *Copyright in Museum Collections.* Washington, DC: American Association of Museums, 1999.

Segal, Terry. "Collections Management: Marking." In Buck and Gilmore, *New Museum Registration Methods,* 65–94.

Shapiro, Michael, S. I. Miller, and Christine Steiner, eds. *A Museum Guide to Copyright and Trademark by the American Association of Museums*. Washington, DC: AAM, 1999.

Simmons, John. "Managing Things: Crafting a Collections Policy." *Museum News*. 83, no. 1 (January/February 2004), 28–31+.

Stephenson, Christie, and Patricia McClung, eds. *Delivering Digital Images: Cultural Heritage Resources for Education*. The Museum Site Licensing Project, Volume 1. Los Angeles: The Getty Information Institute, 1998.

Stone, Sheila M. "Documenting Collections." In Thompson et al., *Manual of Curatorship*, 127–135.

Thompson, John M.A., et al, eds. *Manual of Curatorship: A Guide to Museum Practice*. London: Butterworths, 1984.

Tompkins, William G. "Should Museums Capitalize Their Collections? Or How Much Collateral Is That Caravaggio." *Museum News* 83, no. 1 (January/February 2004), 27.

Ullberg, Allen, and Patricia Ullberg. *Museum Trusteeship*. Washington, DC: AAM, 1981.

Ullberg, Patricia. "What Happened in Greenville: The Need for Codes of Ethics." *Museum News* 60, no. 2 (November–December 1981), 26–29.

Weil, Stephen E. *Beauty and the Beasts: Museums, Art, the Law, and the Market*. Washington, DC: Smithsonian Institution Press, 1983.

Weil, Stephen E., ed. *A Deaccession Reader*. Washington, DC: AAM, 1997.

Weisz, Jackie, Compiler, and Roxana Adams, Series Editor. *Codes of Ethics and Practice of Interest to Museums*. Washington, DC: AAM, 2000.

Williams, Stephen L. "Critical Concepts Concerning Non-Living Collections." *Collections* 1 (2004), 37–66.

Zwiesler, Catherine. "Barcoding." *Spectra* 23, no. 1 (Fall 1995), 18–20.

See also www.AASLH.org./Bookshelf for up-to-date information on collection-related information.

Index

access, 98
accession: definition of, 7; file, 35;
  information, 61

bequests, 29
board action, 34

catalogues: association, 92–93;
  computer, 96; definition of, 8, 81;
  information, 61–62; main entry, 89;
  manual, 89; responsibility for,
  13–14
cataloguing by computer, 82
Chenall, Robert, 85
classification, 84
collections: private, 6; tired, 72
collections management policy,
  10–12
computers: backing up, 137; cost of,
  135; hardware, 131; LANS and
  WANS, 132; security, 136; software,
  126–29; updating, 136
copyright, 26
curator, definition of, 8

data: description, 62; entry, 132;
  historical, 62; management, 62;
  number of fields, 120
data dictionary, 134
deaccessioning, 68–72; of
  undocumented objects, 70–71
digital images, 50
director, 8
documentation: of accessions, 71–72;
  definition of, 8; poor, 14–20

exchange, of accessions, 30

gifts, 27–28; acknowledgement of, 31;
  gift agreement, 28

images, digital and photographic, 93
inventory, 97

ledger, 15, 58; computer-generated, 59;
  manual, 59
loans: condition of, 105; conservation,
  112; deposit, 113; insurance, 109–10;
  loan numbers, 111; loan policy, 103;

185

~

About the Author

Daniel B Reibel has completed a fifty-year career as a curator or director in the museum community. Beginning at the Detroit Historical Museum, he has worked at the Allen County–Fort Wayne Historical Society and the Old Barracks Museum giving him his experience with small museums. He had a twenty-five-year career with the Pennsylvania Historical and Museum Commission as director of Old Economy Village, the Landis Valley Museum, and Washington Crossing Historic Park and as a regional director. He completed his career in museums as a volunteer in the collections department of the Mercer Museum, Bucks County Historical Society.

Along with his wife, Patricia, he collects plumb bobs, a collection that will not conflict with any museum which he may serve. He has worked as an on-site visitor for the MAP program, the Accreditation Commission of the American Association of Museums, and the American Association for State and Local History. He has held offices in several museum associations. He served in the U.S. Marine Corps during the Korean War.